INVENTORS WHO CHANGED THE WORLD

JOHANNES GUTENBERG

THE PRINTER WHO GAVE WORDS TO THE WORLD

STEPHEN FEINSTEIN

MyReportLinks.com Books

an imprint of

Enslow Publishers, Inc.

Box 398, 40 Industrial Road
Berkeley Heights, NJ 07922
USA

MyReportLinks.com Books, an imprint of Enslow Publishers, Inc. MyReportLinks®
is a registered trademark of Enslow Publishers, Inc.

Library of Congress Cataloging-in-Publication Data

Feinstein, Stephen.
  Johannes Gutenberg : the printer who gave words to the world / Stephen Feinstein.
      p. cm. — (Inventors who changed the world)
  Includes bibliographical references and index.
  ISBN-13: 978-1-59845-077-4
  ISBN-10: 1-59845-077-8
  1. Gutenberg, Johann, 1397–1468—Juvenile literature. 2. Printers—Germany—Biography—Juvenile literature.
3. Printing—History—Origin and antecedents—Juvenile literature. I. Title.
  Z126.Z7F45 2007
  686.2092—dc22
                                      2006037535

Printed in the United States of America

10 9 8 7 6 5 4 3 2 1

To Our Readers:
Through the purchase of this book, you and your library gain access to the Report Links that specifically back up this book.
The Publisher will provide access to the Report Links that back up this book and will keep these Report Links up to date on **www.myreportlinks.com** for five years from the book's first publication date.
We have done our best to make sure all Internet addresses in this book were active and appropriate when we went to press. However, the author and the Publisher have no control over, and assume no liability for, the material available on those Internet sites or on other Web sites they may link to.
The usage of the MyReportLinks.com Books Web site is subject to the terms and conditions stated on the Usage Policy Statement on **www.myreportlinks.com**.
A password may be required to access the Report Links that back up this book. The password is found on the bottom of page 4 of this book.
Any comments or suggestions can be sent by e-mail to comments@myreportlinks.com or to the address on the back cover.

♻ Enslow Publishers, Inc. is committed to printing our books on recycled paper. The paper in every book contains between 10% to 30% post-consumer waste (PCW). The cover board on the outside of each book contains 100% PCW. Our goal is to do our part to help young people and the environment too!

Photo Credits: APHA, p. 117; Bowdoin College, p. 11; Bridwell Library, 2007, p. 75; Charles Muller, p. 21; Cornell University Library, p. 59; Cornell University Library Division of Rare and Manuscript Collections, p. 62; Derk Bodde/Columbia University, p. 19; Dr. Karen Carr, Associate Professor of History, Portland State University, p. 27; Educational Broadcasting Corporation, p. 38; Gutenberg Museum-Mainz, p. 68; Harry Ransom Center, pp. 81, 94; Joan Reitz, Haas Instruction Librarian, Western Connecticut State University, p. 102; John H. Lienhard, p. 100; Karakas, p. 54; Library of Congress, pp. 10, 16–17, 36–37, 46, 60–61, 76, 84–85, 91, 110–111, 115; Massachusetts Institute of Technology, p. 35; MyReportLinks.com Books, p. 4; National Diet Library, Japan, p. 44; NPR, p. 13; Perry Castaneda Map Collection, University of Texas, p. 50; Photos.com, pp. 1 (page), 5, 8–9, 30–31, 32–33, 48–49, 52, 57, 66–67, 78–79, 93, 96–97, 106–107; Pious University of the Paper Makers, p. 24; President and Fellows of Harvard College, p. 92; Shutterstock.com, pp. 25, 42–43, 70–71, 73, 98; Springfield Library, p. 101; SUB Goettingen, p. 112; © The British Library Board, pp. 22, 82, 88; The Open University, p. 51; The Paper Project, p. 104; The Schoyen Collection, p. 14; WGBH Educational Foundation, p. 80.

Cover Photo and Illustration: Photos.com (page); Public Domain/Seventeenth century painting of Gutenberg, (portrait).

CONTENTS

MyReportLinks.com Books
Great Books, Great Links, Great for Research!

The Internet sites featured in this book can save you hours of research time. These Internet sites—we call them **"Report Links"**—are constantly changing, but we keep them up to date on our Web site.

When you see this "Approved Web Site" logo, you will know that we are directing you to a great Internet site that will help you with your research.

Give it a try! Type http://www.myreportlinks.com into your browser, click on the series title and enter the password, then click on the book title, and scroll down to the Report Links listed for this book.

The Report Links will bring you to great source documents, photographs, and illustrations. MyReportLinks.com Books save you time, feature Report Links that are kept up to date, and make report writing easier than ever! A complete listing of the Report Links can be found on pages 118–119 at the back of the book.

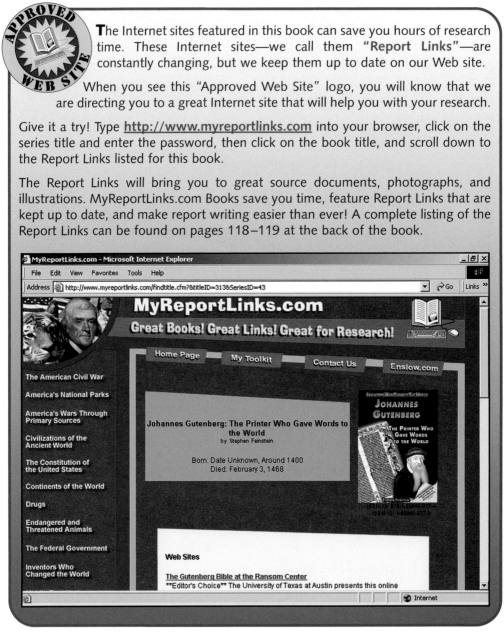

Please see "To Our Readers" on the copyright page for important information about this book, the MyReportLinks.com Web site, and the Report Links that back up this book.

Please enter JGP1885 if asked for a password.

"It is a press, certainly, but a press from which shall flow inexhaustible streams. . . ."

—Johannes Gutenberg

Important Dates

B.C. **1700**—Ancient Cretans are the first known people to have printed images onto stone tablets.

A.D. **105**—Chinese Imperial Counselor Ts'ai Lun is the first to figure out how to make paper.

600—The Chinese invent block printing, using woodblocks to make imprints on paper.

868—The oldest copy of the *Diamond Sutra*, the first known printed book, was dated May 11.

1041—Chinese first to invent movable type, using clay tablets.

1234—Movable type printing is used in Korea.

1398—Johannes Gutenberg is likely born in Mainz, Germany. No one knows his true birthday.

1411—Family flees to Eltville to escape social turmoil in Mainz.

1419—Father, Friele Gensfleisch, dies.

1434—Living in Strasbourg.

1437—Agrees to teach Andreas Dritzehn the precious stones trade.

1438—Forms partnership with Andreas Dritzehn, Hans Riffe, and Andreas Heilmann to produce mirrors for pilgrimage.

1443—Partnership with Riffe and Heilmann ends.

1442—Possible date of earliest example of printing with Gutenberg's movable type.

1448—Gutenberg returns to Mainz.

1450—Borrows money from Johann Fust and begins printing *Ars Grammatica*.

1452—Forms partnership with Fust and begins printing the forty-two-line Bible.

1455 —Loses court case in which all his work and equipment is awarded to Fust just as Bible is nearing completion.

1455 –1457 —Gutenberg borrows money from Konrad Humery and sets up print shop.

1462 —Flees to Eltville because of dangerous political situation in Mainz.

1465 —Returns to Mainz and is granted an annual pension.

1468 —Gutenberg Dies on February 3, in Mainz.

1517 —Printed copies of Martin Luther's 95 Theses spread throughout the Western world.

1836 —Samuel Morse sends the first telegram using his Morse code.

1865 —William Bullock invents a way to print on both sides of a piece of paper.

1873 —Christopher Latham Sholes invents the typewriter.

1951 —UNIVAC is the first computer available for sale.

1977 —Apple Computer releases an affordable home computer.

1994 —Use of the World Wide Web becomes widespread.

SPREADING THE WORD

On October 31, 1517, a German monk and scholar named Martin Luther tacked a document to the door of the Castle Church in Wittenberg, Germany. Luther, a teacher at the University of Wittenberg, believed that the Catholic Church and Pope Leo X were distorting Christ's message and incorrectly preaching religion. Luther was especially angry at Pope Leo's decision to raise money by selling indulgences, or church-approved documents that essentially meant that anyone who was willing to pay could avoid punishment for their sins. The document, called "Disputation of Martin Luther on the Power and Efficacy of Indulgences," commonly known as The 95 Theses, outlined the reasons why Luther thought the church and the Pope were wrong. Luther invited the public to join him in a debate on the issue.

Luther obviously knew that his 95 Theses would spark a heated discussion among the people who read it. That, after all, was his goal.

CHAPTER

1

However, he probably never imagined that his written assault on indulgences and the church's leadership would help launch the Protestant Reformation. This sixteenth-century movement reshaped the Catholic Church and reorganized religion in Western Europe.

Not long after Luther posted his paper on that church door, someone copied it and took it to a local printer and had them make additional copies. And, in what was then thought to be an incredibly short period of time, Luther's revolutionary ideas had been read and talked about all over Europe.

"The theses . . . were said to be known throughout Germany in a fortnight [two weeks] and throughout Europe in a month . . . the printing presses transformed the field of communications and fathered an international revolt. It was a revolution."[1]

Imagine what might have happened if Martin Luther had written his attack on the church fifty years earlier than he did—before Johannes Gutenberg developed his printing press. Luther's 95 Theses might have made a splash in Wittenberg, or maybe they would even have been talked about in a nearby

Martin Luther was a German monk who disagreed with certain policies of the Roman Catholic Church. To voice his displeasure, he wrote the 95 Theses which led to the Protestant Reformation.

town or two. But the movement known as the Protestant Reformation? It might not have happened because the information probably would not have spread quickly enough.

* * * * *

If you could travel back in time one thousand years to Europe during the Middle Ages, you would find yourself in a very strange world. Virtually everything that we take for granted today—from transportation to communication to electricity to indoor plumbing—was nonexistent.

If you wanted to speak to a friend on a nearby street or in a nearby town, you walked. Or, if you were fortunate, you owned a horse and could ride.

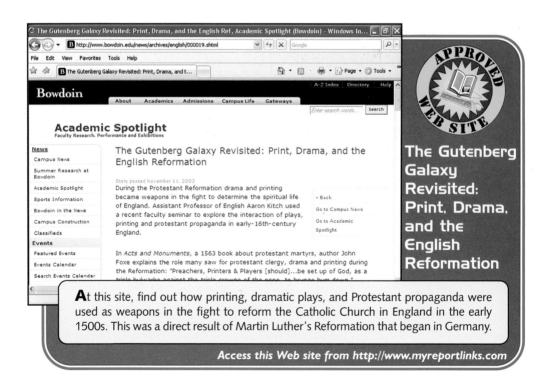

The Gutenberg Galaxy Revisited: Print, Drama, and the English Reformation

At this site, find out how printing, dramatic plays, and Protestant propaganda were used as weapons in the fight to reform the Catholic Church in England in the early 1500s. This was a direct result of Martin Luther's Reformation that began in Germany.

Access this Web site from http://www.myreportlinks.com

The towns themselves were small, and even the biggest cities had no more than about twenty thousand people living in them. Regardless, news traveled very slowly. It could take at least a day for information to reach the next town. Candles were the only source of artificial light and they were expensive, so only the wealthy lit their homes. No one had a toilet. People went to the bathroom in something called a chamber pot, the contents of which were often dumped out the window and onto the street.

The dirty conditions of the Middle Ages certainly helped spread the plague. This was a disastrous disease known as the Black Death because of the purplish or black spots that appeared on a victim's skin. The plague swept across Europe in the fourteenth century and killed between 25 and 40 million people, about one third of Europe's population.

➡ WIDESPREAD IGNORANCE AND SUPERSTITION

Needless to say, there was nothing like the instant communication or constant news that we have today. There was no such thing as a newspaper, magazine, or the Internet, not even leaflets or posters to speak of. What news there was spread by word of mouth. And in general, the information that was available in those days was available only to those people who could read—and few people could. Mainly, only people who were wealthy

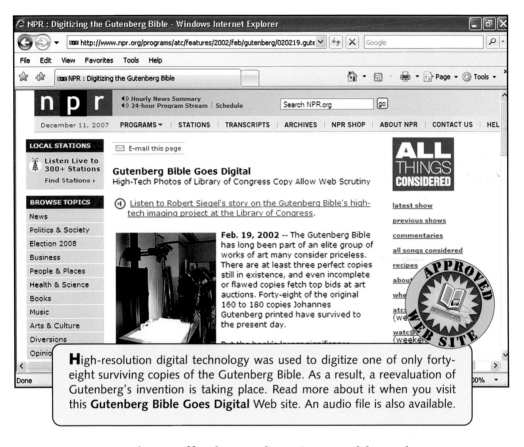

High-resolution digital technology was used to digitize one of only forty-eight surviving copies of the Gutenberg Bible. As a result, a reevaluation of Gutenberg's invention is taking place. Read more about it when you visit this **Gutenberg Bible Goes Digital** Web site. An audio file is also available.

enough to afford an education could read; most people were illiterate. As a result, most people were ignorant about what was occurring in even the next town.

Because most people were not educated and could not read, they did not know much about the world around them. Even relatively common things like thunder and lightning scared people because they had no idea what caused them. In the Middle Ages, people believed that thunder and lightning were the result of battles between evil spirits.

People relied on the church and its teachings and on legends and myths to help them understand the world. Superstition and magic, not science, provided answers. In fact, virtually all forms of scientific investigation were discouraged by the church. Educated people risked the loss of their property and even their lives if they announced a discovery contrary to Church doctrine.

➡ BOOKS PRODUCED BY SCRIBES

Most people in the Middle Ages lived their entire life without ever seeing a book, much less reading one. But books did exist, as did libraries and universities. They were, however, for the benefit of the small, educated class of the wealthy.

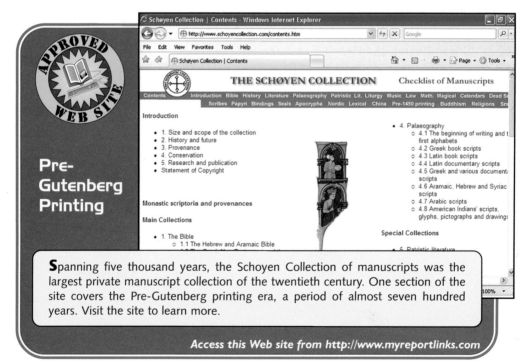

Pre-Gutenberg Printing

Spanning five thousand years, the Schøyen Collection of manuscripts was the largest private manuscript collection of the twentieth century. One section of the site covers the Pre-Gutenberg printing era, a period of almost seven hundred years. Visit the site to learn more.

Access this Web site from http://www.myreportlinks.com

Throughout the Middle Ages, priests and monks in thousands of monasteries kept learning alive in Europe. The small number of books that were produced were all handwritten by monks working as scribes. In the seclusion of their monasteries, the scribes made hand-lettered copies of the Bible and other religious works. They would also produce copies of nonreligious works, such as the epic poem *Beowulf* and Geoffrey Chaucer's *Canterbury Tales.*

It took an incredible amount of time to produce a book. The monks worked six hours a day, only during daylight, in an area of the monastery called the scriptorium. Working by candlelight was too dangerous—the risk of fire was too great.

According to writer John Man, "a scribe would be hard pressed to copy more than two high-quality, densely packed pages a week (one 1,272-page commentary on the Bible took two scribes five years—1453–58—to complete)."[2] And because so many hours of labor were required to produce a single manuscript, books were very expensive—so much so that they were usually loosely chained to library shelves. This way, they could be opened and read but not removed from the room.

Consistency from book to book was another problem. Everyone makes mistakes, and scribes sometimes erred, which meant that copies of the same book would often be different. On occasion,

In Europe, most of the first books were made by scribes who were most often Catholic monks. This is an engraving of Jean Mielot, a monk and scribe who worked in medieval times.

scribes grew bored with copying and purposely made changes to the material.

For the most part, the books that the scribes produced were for the Catholic Church because monasteries maintained their own libraries. But wealthy members of royal courts kept their own libraries and they also donated large amounts to the monastery in exchange for the monks to produce books. These wealthy nobles saw books as status symbols and believed that owning them proved their owners were people of culture and learning.

The scribes used quill pens, made from a bird's feather, and ink. They wrote on parchment, a paper-like material that was made from the dried skins of goats or sheep. The best parchment, called vellum, was made from calfskin. The scribes wrote in Latin, and their elegant writing was known as calligraphy. After they wrote the words on the parchment, they decorated the pages with elaborate designs and borders. Some of the pages included miniature scenes painted in bright colors. Capital letters were decorated with designs in gold leaf. The finished pages were called illuminated manuscripts.

Calligraphy is still used today. Usually, fancy invitations or announcements will be decorated with calligraphy on envelopes and cards. Although, oftentimes people use computer fonts that look very much like calligraphy and do not have to learn the skill themselves.

→ Early Developments in Printing and Papermaking

Johannes Gutenberg developed a process that made it relatively easy to print many copies of a book or document, but he did not invent printing. Some method of printing words or images on a surface has been around almost as long as people have been writing. In 1908, archeologists discovered a clay disc in Crete, Greece, believed to date from about 1700 B.C. Stamped into the clay are 241 images that were embedded there with hard metal stamps. Elsewhere, scribes in ancient Egypt used wooden blocks to print hieroglyphs onto tiles.

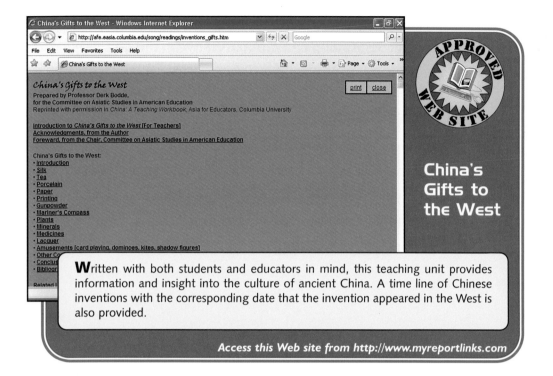

China's Gifts to the West - Windows Internet Explorer

http://afe.easia.columbia.edu/song/readings/inventions_gifts.htm

File   Edit   View   Favorites   Tools   Help

China's Gifts to the West

Page ▼ Tools ▼

China's Gifts to the West
Prepared by Professor Derk Bodde,
for the Committee on Asiatic Studies in American Education
Reprinted with permission in *China: A Teaching Workbook*, Asia for Educators, Columbia University

Introduction to *China's Gifts to the West* [For Teachers]
Acknowledgments, from the Author
Foreward, from the Chair, Committee on Asiatic Studies in American Education

China's Gifts to the West:
· Introduction
· Silk
· Tea
· Porcelain
· Paper
· Printing
· Gunpowder
· Mariner's Compass
· Plants
· Minerals
· Medicines
· Lacquer
· Amusements [card playing, dominoes, kites, shadow figures]
· Other Co
· Conclus
· Bibliogr

Related I

print   close

China's Gifts to the West

Written with both students and educators in mind, this teaching unit provides information and insight into the culture of ancient China. A time line of Chinese inventions with the corresponding date that the invention appeared in the West is also provided.

Access this Web site from http://www.myreportlinks.com

APPROVED WEB SITE

The ancient Cretans and Egyptians were unable to print extensively. There were so many characters in each language, that it was impractical to print a long message.

The ancient Romans actually came closest to making the breakthrough into full-scale printing. Metalworkers invented and used movable type to create short messages on the lead pipes that fed fountains, baths, and private homes. The messages recorded the name of the emperor or the municipal official who had ordered and paid for the expansion of the water system. Though their method was strangely similar to the one that Gutenberg would invent more than one thousand years later, the Romans used their system sparingly and the technology disappeared with the fall of the Roman Empire in the fifth century.

→ MAKING PAPER

Paper, an essential part of printing, was developed in China in A.D. 105 by the imperial counselor Ts'ai Lun. According to official Chinese records, Ts'ai Lun "conceived the idea of making paper from the bark of trees, hemp waste, old rags, and fish nets."[3] The Chinese then developed a simple form of printing, which involved carving inscriptions in stone slabs. Moistened paper was pressed onto the inscription stones and then the paper was brushed with ink. The markings left by the stone-cut characters stood out white against the blackened paper.

By A.D. 600, the Chinese had developed block printing, the technique of using a carved block of wood to make imprints on paper. But, like copying a book by hand, block printing required a lot of work. An entire page of text and illustrations first had to be carved into the wood with each character or illustration cut in reverse by removing all the surrounding wood. The raised lines that were left were then inked. Sheets of paper were then pressed onto the blocks with a bamboo stick, bone, or dry brush to produce an impression. The resulting print was unable to be changed, with black writing on a white background. The oldest known surviving Chinese printed document is from the Wu Zetian period (A.D. 684 to A.D. 705).

The earliest known printed book, the *Diamond Sutra,* was found in China in the Cave of the Thousand Buddhas near Tun-huang in Kansu Province. It is made up of six sheets of text, pasted together to form a roll, with a one-page, woodcut illustration. It is dated May 11, 868. In 1041, the Chinese developed a system of movable type using baked clay tablets. Then in 1314, a local judge named Wang Chen used nearly sixty thousand movable wooden type characters to print a book about agriculture.

By the eighth century, Buddhist monks had spread the art of papermaking and block printing

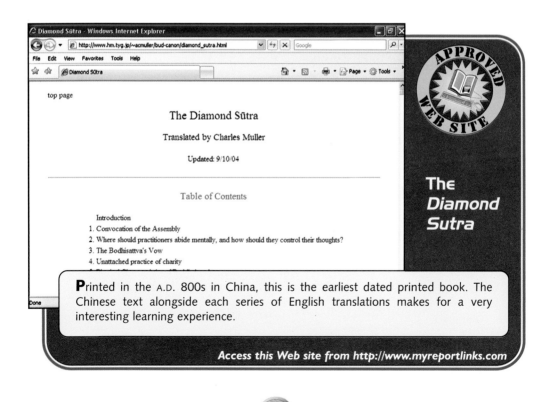

Printed in the A.D. 800s in China, this is the earliest dated printed book. The Chinese text alongside each series of English translations makes for a very interesting learning experience.

Access this Web site from http://www.myreportlinks.com

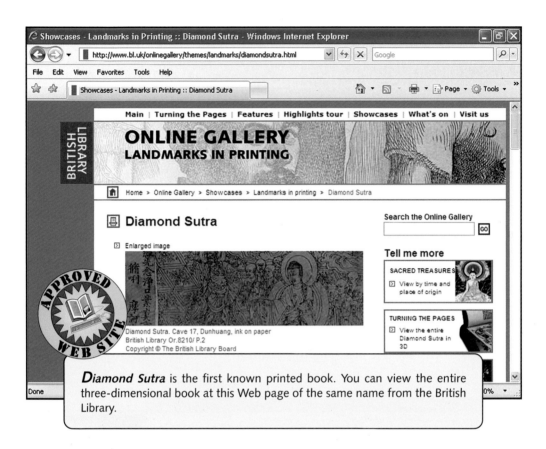

Diamond Sutra. Cave 17, Dunhuang, ink on paper
British Library Or.8210/ P.2
Copyright © The British Library Board

Diamond Sutra is the first known printed book. You can view the entire three-dimensional book at this Web page of the same name from the British Library.

from China to Korea and Japan. The Japanese Empress Shotoku, who reigned from A.D. 748 to 769, ordered a million copies of Buddhist prayers. For six years, over 150 men produced them using block printing.

Despite their many contributions to the craft, the Chinese did not make printing a widespread practice. The Chinese language, which is made up of at least forty thousand characters, or ideographs, was far too complex for practical typographic printing. And the quality of woodblock printing was no match for the high standards of Chinese calligraphy. And, in reality, there was no great incentive for the Chinese to overcome such difficulties, primarily because there was no huge public demand for reading matter. Printing was a tool used to make permanent records of official decrees. And official communications could more easily be written by hand.

In contrast to Chinese, European languages had relatively simple alphabets of twenty-four letters. Thus, they were much better suited to the revolutionary movable type printing technology that Gutenberg would invent.

⇒KOREAN CONTRIBUTIONS

In the year 1234, a Korean named Chwe Yun-ui invented a system of movable-type printing. In 1418, Emperor Sejong, who promoted printing, came to the throne in Korea. During his thirty-two-year reign, about 150 books were produced by the method of movable-type printing. Sejong sought to revolutionize Korean language and printing, developing an alphabet derived from Chinese script. Characters were engraved in wood, molds of porcelain paste were made from these models, and in these molds metal type was cast.

The Correct Sounds for the Instruction of the People, the fruit of Sejong's labor, was published in 1443. In his introduction, he wrote, "Among the ignorant, there have been many who, having

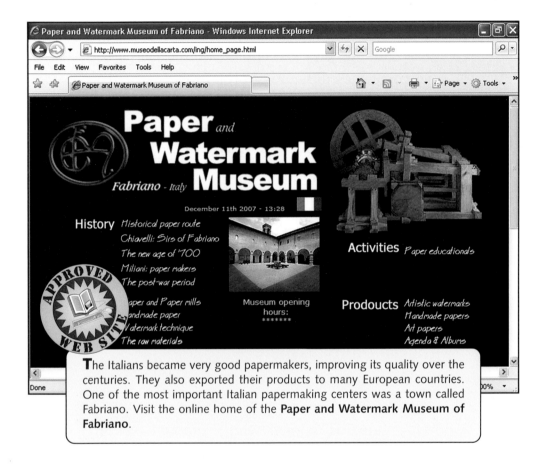

Paper and Watermark Museum of Fabriano - Windows Internet Explorer

http://www.museodellacarta.com/ing/home_page.html

File   Edit   View   Favorites   Tools   Help

Paper and Watermark Museum of Fabriano

Paper *and*
Watermark
Fabriano - Italy **Museum**

December 11th 2007 - 13:28

History   *Historical paper route*
Chiavelli: Sirs of Fabriano
The new age of '700
Miliani: paper makers
The post-war period
...aper and Paper mills
...andmade paper
...atermark technique
The raw materials

Activities *Paper educationals*

Museum opening
hours:
****

Prodoucts *Artistic watermarks*
Handmade papers
Art papers
Agenda & Albums

The Italians became very good papermakers, improving its quality over the centuries. They also exported their products to many European countries. One of the most important Italian papermaking centers was a town called Fabriano. Visit the online home of the **Paper and Watermark Museum of Fabriano**.

something to put into words, have in the end been unable to express their feelings. I have been distressed by this, and have newly designed a script of twenty-eight letters, which I wish to have everyone practice at their ease." Chinese took years to master, but Hangul (Great Script), as this new script became known, was something "a wise man may acquaint himself with before the morning is over . . . even the sound of the winds, the cry of the crane and the barking of the dog—all may be written."[4]

quari: o omnes mūdani. Adq̄rite hūc vnū
lapidē preciosum: recondite in arca cordis
hoc nomen gloriosum triū syllabaꝝ. Ma/
ria. Et eritis securi in omni periculo: habe/
bitis auxilium in omni necessitate ꝁ angu/
stia ꝁ psperitatē in omi salubꝛi optato. Ail
enim est mali qͦ non remoueat. Ail boni
qͦ non obtineat. Aonum priuilegium
quia hoc nomen est sūme confortatiuum si
homo aduertat: qꝛ nullus sperauit in ea ꝁ
confusus est. nullus inuocare potuit sic: vt
derelictus sit dūmodo bene inuocauerit. iu
xta illud Esa.ꝗꝗ. Quis ambulauit in tene/
bꝛis ꝁ nō est lumē ei id est maria ī auxiliū:
q.d.nullus. Unde omīs homo in ea spem
ponere habꝛ: qꝛ vt canit ecclesia. Ipa est re
gina misericordie vita dulcedo ꝁ spes no/
stra. Et ipa est mater gratie ꝁ mater miseri
cordie que ab hoste protegit: in hora moꝛ/
tis suscipit. O tu qui times a piculo dāna/
tionis recordare huius nominis. quia ma/
ria maris stella interpꝛatur. Si maris stel
la ergo ad portū salutis deducens in h̄ ma
ri magno ꝁ spacioso. Hinc Bern. O hō se
curū habes accessuꝛ ꝁ ad deū vbi maꝛ stat
pro te ante filium: ꝁ filius ante patrē. Fi/
lius ostēdit patri latus ꝁ vulnera. Mater
ostēdit filio pectus ꝁ vbera: nulla poterit eē
repulsa vbi tot concurrūt amoꝛis insignia.
An nō ergo cōfortaris quotiens nominis
eius recordaris. Dicit idem Bern. de no/
mine iesus: qͦ ꝁ de nomine marie accipere
valemꝰ. Hinc ꝓpheta dauid ait. Sperēt
in te qui nouerūt nomen tuum. Decimū
priuilegiū: qꝛ nomē marie est gratiossimū.
Interpꝛatur enim maria illuminatrix scz
lumine gratie: ꝁ pfecto nomē marie gratio
sum est: qꝛ ipa brī ꝩgo est mater grē. Ao
ta autez q̄ Pm quincꝫ litteras huius nois
maria ꝙntuplicem gratiā peccatoꝛes conse
quūtur ꝑ hoc nomē: quas quidē grās hoc
nome significare videꝛ. Prima lꝛa M de/
notat misericordiā diuinā. Scͦa A deno/
tat amoꝛem supernoꝛ ꝁ eius accensionem.
Tertia R significat remissionē peccatoꝛū.
Quarta lꝛa J denotat illuminationē ex in
fusione iustificātis gratie. Quita littera A
denotat adquisitionē vicꝫ meritoꝛ ꝁ pmio
rum. Hinc Bern. in sermone. Si criminis
imanitate turbatus: si conscientie feditate

confusus: si iudiciꝝ horroꝛe pterritus: si ba
rathro desperatiōis absoꝛptus. Mariam
cogita: maria inuoca. Et sic in temetipo ex
periri poteris q̄ merito dictū sit nome vir/
ginis maria. Hec ille. Undecima preroga
gatiua nois marie est: qꝛ est nomen dulcissi
mū. Unde canit ecclia. Salue regīa ꝁ mise
ricordie vita dulcedo ꝁ spes nostra. Unde
ipa est clemētissima regina: vita spes ꝁ dul
cedo nostra: sequiꝛ q̄ nomē eius est dulcissi
mū. Aimirū ex noīe marie nisi assit impedi
mentum in hoīe: tanta dulcedo cordi deuo
to infundiꝛ: q̄ mentis affectū magis ac ma
gis afficit nec satiari potest pꝛe desiderio:
qͦ testaꝛ Ecci.c.ꝗꝗꝗ. dicens in psona eius
Spūs inquit meus sup mel dulcis: ꝁ here
ditas mea sup mel ꝁ fauum: memoꝛia mea
in generationes seculoꝛ. Qui edunt me ad
huc esurient scꝫ ꝑ desiderio. Esa.ꝗꝗ. Aot
men tuū in desiderio aie. Aota autem q̄
nomen marie dulcoꝛez infert. Primo visui
Ps. Letificabis me cum vultu tuo delecta
tiones in dextera tua vscꝫ in finem. Scͦo
auditu. Can. ij. Sonet vox tua in auribus
meis. Uox em tua dulcis ꝁ facies tua deco
ra. Tertio dulcoꝛem infert gustui. Cantic.
ij. Fructus eius dulcis gutturi meo. Quar
to olfatui Ecci.ꝗꝗꝗ. Quasi myrrha ele/
cta dedi suauitatē odoꝛis. Et ibidez. Ego
quasi vitis fructificaui suauitatem odoꝛis.
Quinto dulcoꝛez infert cordis medull. vn
Can. vij. Pone me vt signaculū super coꝛ
tuum. Et ps. Gustate ꝁ videte qm suauis
est dūs scꝫ in maria. ꝛc. O vtinam fidelis
anima aliquando nouisses. experientia cer
ta: quia vt canit ecclia. Uere demens pia ꝁ
dulcis est maria. Duodecima prerogati
ua: quia nomen marie est efficacia mirabi/
lissimū. Mirabiles em efficere habꝛ fruct
salutiferos vt in parte prima articulo vlti/
mo patuit. Quis denicꝫ sufficiēter extima
re poterit quanta a principio mundi mira/
cula facta sint ad nomen marie ꝁ eiꝰ inuo/
cationem. Si enim (vt dicit ps.) Mirabi/
lis deus in sanctis suis: q̄ mirabilis sup o/
mnes in maria que est omnium sanctissi/
ma ꝁ domina. Cui vt dicit Bern. data est
omnis potestas in celo ꝁ in terra: v ꝁ quic/
quid voluerit valeat efficere. Ut aū ꝁ magꝫ
clarescat mirabilis efficacia nomini s marie

There would not be a printing revolution in Korea either. "The men of learning opposed Sejong's alphabet because it was not Chinese. They said it was too easy."[5] Also, there was apparently too much resistance to abandoning the Chinese language in favor of Sejong's Great Script. So Hangul was used for only a few of the Emperor's pet projects and for Buddhist literature. Oddly enough, at about the same time that Sejong was introducing his new language, Gutenberg was experimenting with his printing press in Germany.

A "Book Crisis" in Europe

Eventually, paper made its way to Europe, reaching Spain in the twelfth century. However, European paper differed from Chinese paper. The paper the Chinese used was thin and absorbent and could only be used on one side because marks from one side would show through to the other. Europeans needed a thicker paper for their quill pens, so they hardened theirs with animal glue, making it possible for them to write and print on both sides.

Although, while Asian paper came from trees, the most common sources for paper in Europe were linen and cotton rags and flax. The spread of paper in Europe in the fourteenth century "was made possible by a sudden huge increase in the availability of inexpensive recyclable rags: the heaps of unwearable clothing left by victims of various plagues."[6]

It was not just the old clothing that aided the start of printing in Europe. By the A.D. 1300, the continent was undergoing tremendous change. For example, towns were growing and trade between them was increasing, which in turn meant that people needed more information about events and things that were happening in other areas. This period in history came to be called the Renaissance, which comes from the Latin word meaning "rebirth."

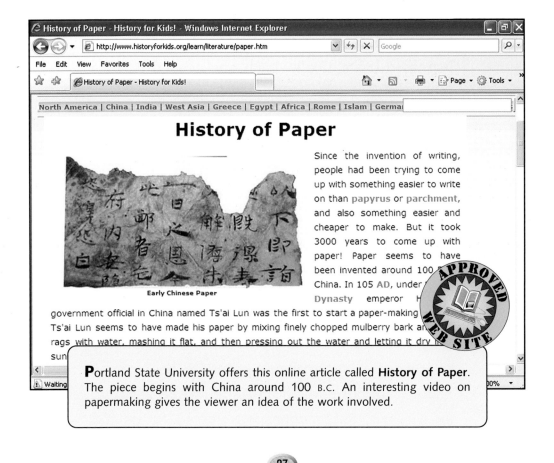

History of Paper - History for Kids! - Windows Internet Explorer

http://www.historyforkids.org/learn/literature/paper.htm

Google

File   Edit   View   Favorites   Tools   Help

History of Paper - History for Kids!

Page ▾   Tools ▾

North America | China | India | West Asia | Greece | Egypt | Africa | Rome | Islam | Germa

History of Paper

Early Chinese Paper

Since the invention of writing, people had been trying to come up with something easier to write on than papyrus or parchment, and also something easier and cheaper to make. But it took 3000 years to come up with paper! Paper seems to have been invented around 100 China. In 105 AD, under Dynasty emperor

government official in China named Ts'ai Lun was the first to start a paper-making Ts'ai Lun seems to have made his paper by mixing finely chopped mulberry bark ar rags with water, mashing it flat, and then pressing out the water and letting it dry sun

APPROVED WEB SITE

Portland State University offers this online article called **History of Paper**. The piece begins with China around 100 B.C. An interesting video on papermaking gives the viewer an idea of the work involved.

In general, there was a rebirth of people's interest and achievement in the arts, sciences, and global exploration. Universities had been established in Paris, Bologna, and other European cities, which resulted in an increased demand for books. Paper was more readily available and less expensive, and as a result books were becoming more affordable. They were no longer just available to the wealthy. At the same time, nobles and other wealthy Europeans wanted more books and were eager to expand their collections. They were especially interested in purchasing personal books of psalms, called psalters. Meanwhile, the number of churches and monasteries across Europe had increased dramatically. Each one needed its own Bible, prayer books, and books of psalms.

Also by A.D. 1300, the process of block printing had reached Europe and Europeans quickly mastered the new technique. Entire pages of books such as the *Poor Man's Bible* were cut on a wooden block and then printed on paper. But scribes in the monasteries could not keep up with the demand. Even with the help of block printing, it still took a long time to produce a book.

The increase in the amount of available paper combined with the onset of the Renaissance and the knowledge of block printing created a "book crisis." There were not enough books to fill the demand. As a result, bookmaking was forced to expand beyond the monastery walls. Bookmaking shops sprang up in Paris and other cities and university towns. Bookmakers came up with more efficient methods of book production, which usually involved a division of labor. Scribes became specialized—one might do only body text, another would only do capitals, and still another would work only on illuminations. Even as bookmakers streamlined their processes, education was improving across the continent and the literacy rate was quickly rising. Soon there were just too many people who wanted books and not enough books. Supply could still not meet demand.

According to author H. G. Wells, by the end of the 1300s in Germany, paper had become:

> Abundant and cheap enough for the printing of books to be a practicable business proposition. Thereupon printing followed naturally and necessarily, and the intellectual life of the world entered upon a new and far more vigorous phase. It ceased to be a little trickle from mind to mind; it became a broad flood, in which thousands and, presently, scores and hundreds of thousands of minds participated.[7]

In other words, the world was ready for Johannes Gutenberg to create his invention.

JOHANNES GUTENBERG: THE EARLY YEARS

Very little is known about the life of Johannes Gutenberg. Mostly, we have records of court cases in which Gutenberg was involved. Even still, historians have closely examined records from the German cities of Strasbourg and Mainz and collected all relevant facts from the records. They have used that information to make educated guesses to fill in the gaps in the recorded information.

GUTENBERG'S BIRTHPLACE

Johannes Gutenberg was born in Mainz sometime between 1394 and 1404. Most believe he was born in one of three years: 1398, 1399, or 1400. Mainz is on the Rhine River not far from where the Main and Rhine rivers converge in western Germany. In the Middle Ages, Mainz was part of the Holy Roman Empire. At the time of Gutenberg's birth, the city was a busy port along the Rhine River. The Rhine was the main trade route through

CHAPTER
2

Europe, and Mainz was one of the continent's richest cities. The merchants of Mainz were busy trafficking goods on the docks and boats were constantly loading and unloading cargo.

The town's economy was driven by merchants and craftsmen (or artisans). As in other towns during medieval times, they belonged to a guild. This was an organized group of people who worked in the same trade, set up similar to today's trade unions. Guild members joined together for their mutual protection, profit, and assistance. Among the town's thirty-four guilds were groups of metalworkers, goldsmiths, painters, rope makers, shoemakers, carpenters, leather workers, butchers, and bakers. The guilds were powerful, enforcing standards of quality and controlling all prices and wages. Because most guilds controlled the distribution of raw materials for their specific trade, it was almost impossible for a craftsman to work without the permission of the guild.

Mainz was governed by an archbishop of the Roman Catholic Church. The Archbishop of Mainz was a powerful individual who held a leading position in the electoral consortium.

Johannes Gutenberg was born into a wealthy and influential family. This street is in the town of Gutenberg, Germany, near the city of Mainz where Johannes Gutenberg grew up.

Beginning in the year 1257, this group had the responsibility of electing and announcing the German king. The Archbishop of Mainz also had the right to mint gold coins to be used as money (the city was given the Latin name *Aurea Moguntia,* which means Golden Mainz). As a result, many highly skilled metal craftsmen and goldsmiths flocked to Mainz to find work.

GUTENBERG'S FAMILY

Johannes Gutenberg was the third child of Friele Gensfleisch and his second wife, Else Wirich. The family was quite wealthy, owning a house in Mainz and an estate in Eltville, six miles (ten kilometers) downriver. Friele was a patrician, or a person descended from the nobility of the region. As a member of the local aristocracy, he served as one of the four master accountants of the city of Mainz. He was also involved in the cloth trade. Else was the daughter of a wealthy merchant. The estate in Eltville came from her side of the family.

Interestingly, when Johannes was a child, his name was Johannes Gensfleisch. In the Middle Ages, it was customary for a house to have a name. And it was customary for family members to use the name of their house as their last name. Gensfleisch, meaning "gooseflesh," was the name of one of the two houses owned by Frilo, the

View an online handbook to help inventors learn about the business of inventing, with information on raising capital and applying for patents. A searchable "Inventor of the Week" archives is available, as well as games, inventor biographies, and links to other resources.

Access this Web site from http://www.myreportlinks.com

great-great-grandfather of Johannes Gutenberg. Yet the family home in Mainz was named Gutenberg. Why then was Johannes's last name Gensfleisch? The reason probably has to do with the history of Mainz during the fourteenth century.

For over three hundred years during the Middle Ages, Mainz had been a popular destination for European Jews. The Gutenberg house was called the "Judenberg" or Jewish Hill. But in 1282, a pogrom against Jewish people, or an organized massacre, took place in Mainz. Many Jews were killed and dozens of properties that had been owned by Jews were grabbed by other powerful landowners. One of these properties, the Gutenberg, was eventually acquired by Frilo.

In 1347, the bubonic plague, or Black Death, reached Europe. The next year, it raced across Europe, reaching Germany and the cities along the Rhine in 1348. The Italian author Giovanni Boccaccio, writing about the plague in *The Decameron,* said that "This scourge had implanted so great a terror in the hearts of men and women that brothers abandoned brothers, uncles their nephews, sisters their brothers, and in many cases wives deserted their husbands. But even worse, . . . fathers and mothers refused to nurse and assist their own children."[1]

In the cities along the Rhine, terrified townspeople who had no understanding of how the plague was actually spread did not

The house owned by Gutenberg's family was formerly the estate of a wealthy Jewish family. Many Orthodox Jews were also scribes and remained so long after the invention of the printing press. Shlomo Washadi is shown here working as a scribe in the late 1930s.

look far for a scapegoat. Rumors spread that the Jews had poisoned the wells and that they were to blame.[2] In one city after another, Jews were killed, often burned alive. On St. Valentine's Day 1348, chronicler Jakob Twinger von Königshofen reported that "the Jews were burned in Strasbourg in their churchyard on a wooden scaffolding. Furthermore, anything owed to the Jews was regarded as settled. Any cash owned by the Jews was taken by the council and distributed among the craft trades. Thus it was that the Jews

Background information, clues, evidence, and interviews make up this online examination of the bubonic plague called *Secrets of the Dead: Mystery of the Black Death*. A short video on the subject is also available.

were burned in Strasbourg and in the same year in all the cities along the Rhine."[3]

When the plague reached Mainz, about ten thousand people, at least half the townspeople died. Over the course of the next two decades, the plague swept through the Rhine cities at least twice more. The population of Mainz dropped from twenty thousand to about six thousand, the number of guilds from fifty to thirty-four.

Given the consequences of the plague and the horrific acts of anti-Semitism its spread brought about in Mainz, it is not surprising that for several generations the Gensfleisch family chose not to link their family name to the house called Jewish Hill.

⇒ GUTENBERG'S EDUCATION

There are no records of Johannes Gutenberg's early education, but as a child of a patrician family, he most likely had the same sort of education as other children of that social class. The patrician families of Mainz sent their sons to schools in convents, monasteries, and cathedrals. Johannes probably received his early education at one of these schools. He was obviously taught to read and write, and he would have studied Latin. He would have spent much of his time learning prayers and Bible passages by heart, also in Latin. In addition, he probably learned the Arabic system of numerals.

Unlike children from patrician families, the sons of tradesmen and craftsmen were educated in the apprentice system, meaning they were trained in a particular trade or craft. A boy was apprenticed for five to nine years to a master to learn the trade or craft. In return, the boy had to work for the master until such time as he was ready to be advanced to the grade of journeyman. As a journeyman, the boy worked for wages on a day-to-day basis. To become a master and thus, run a business, hire journeymen, and teach apprentices, a journeyman was required to produce a top-quality, test piece of work that qualified as a "masterpiece." In many places, the wealthier families gradually took control of the guilds. Many craftsmen without influence were unable to become masters, and had to spend the rest of their lives as journeymen.

⊜ LEARNING TO MINT

Johannes's father Friele and his uncle were officials at the Archbishop of Mainz's mint. Friele's title was "Companion of the Mint." Most likely that is where Johannes learned the art of precision metalwork in the production of coins. At the mint, master metalworkers and goldsmiths trained apprentices to become journeyman and, eventually, masters. Although he trained at the mint, Johannes did not have to serve as an apprentice because of his father's position. And, even so, Johannes was not eligible for membership in a guild because he was a member of the patrician class.

While training, Johannes learned various essential metalworking skills, including the techniques of molding and casting, and the cutting of steel punches used to make coin dies. He also learned how metals behaved at different temperatures, and what their melting points were. He learned the properties of various alloys. He even became skilled in the stamping of gold. Later, as he struggled to develop his movable metal type, Johannes would put the skills he learned at the mint to good use.

⇒ Upper Education

Johannes probably attended a university after his training at the mint. Many sons of the patrician families of Mainz attended the University of Erfurt. There is an entry in the enrollment forms of 1419 and 1420 for a Johannes de Altavilla (Eltville). However, there's no way of knowing if that was Johannes Gutenberg or not.

As a university student, Johannes would definitely have studied grammar, rhetoric, logic, and possibly music, arithmetic, geometry, and astronomy. In the Middle Ages, grammar was considered to be the foundation of all learning. Since grammar books were scarce, teachers would read a question from a book. The students would memorize and

For many years, the Archbishop of Mainz, a high-ranking official in the Catholic Church, essentially ran the city. Pictured here is the cathedral in Mainz.

GUTENBERG IN STRASBOURG

In 1419, while Johannes was likely studying at the University of Erfurt, his father died. There seems to have been a dispute involving the estate, and Johannes's name is mentioned in a court document from 1420. This must have started Johannes thinking about what he would do when he finished his studies.

EXILE FROM MAINZ

Home in Mainz in 1420, Gutenberg faced an uncertain future. Although he adopted Gutenberg as his last name after his father died, that was about all his father passed on to him. He inherited neither property nor a fortune. He could not even move into the Gutenberg house because his older brother and his family were living there, forcing their mother into a smaller house.

By this time, Johannes Gutenberg had learned enough about metalworking to start his own coin-making business, but, as

CHAPTER

3

would be the case in the future, he lacked the financial resources to strike out on his own. While there is no record of what Johannes Gutenberg did for the next ten years, it seems reasonable to assume that he found a way to earn a living as a goldsmith. After all, expertise in coin making was in demand and Gutenberg had connections at the mint through his uncle and departed father.

During the decade of the 1420s, the city of Mainz faced increasingly difficult economic conditions. The town council was dominated by guild members who demanded higher taxes from the patricians. The patricians sought to avoid taxes by retreating to their country estates. The city was quickly going bankrupt. The ambitious Gutenberg concluded there was no future for him in Mainz. He wanted to start a business and hoped to find a town with a more promising economy.

→ SETTLING IN STRASBOURG

Gutenberg left Mainz and settled in Strasbourg, a thriving city about 125 miles (200 kilometers) up the

inventing a practical way to mass-produce books could make him very rich. He also felt that his experimentation with printing must be carried out in secret. If he were to benefit from his work, then his rivals must not learn about what he was up to until he had established a successful printing business.

⮕ SETTING UP SHOP

Gutenberg's first step was to find a location where he could set up his business. He decided that St. Arbogast, a little village named after a local monastery, was perfect. It was close to Strasbourg, only a few miles away up the Ill River, yet it was far enough to afford Gutenberg the seclusion and privacy he needed. Here he could work, conduct business, and experiment with printing in secrecy.

Gutenberg rented a house and hired Lorenz Beildeck and his wife as servants. He set up his workshop and continued his business of cutting and polishing precious stones. In 1437, a wealthy man named Andreas Dritzehn expressed an interest in learning the precious-stone trade—and he was willing to pay for the privilege. Gutenberg agreed to teach him.

That same year, Gutenberg became involved in another court case. A local woman, Ennelin zur Yserin Thüre, claimed that Gutenberg had promised to marry her. Gutenberg denied it, arguing that he was too involved in his work to even consider marriage. Ennelin's mother Ellewibel was outraged and sued Gutenberg for breach of promise. She brought a witness, Claus Schott, a local shoemaker, to the Church court, where the case was heard. According to court records, Gutenberg became so angry that he called Schott, "A miserable wretch who lives by cheating and lying!"[2]

Charlemagne was an ▶ *emperor who founded the Holy Roman Empire in A.D. 800. People would make a pilgrimage to Aachen to view his tomb and collection of holy relics every seven years. Gutenberg had an idea to make mirrors for the travelers, a popular item to bring there.*

Schott demanded to be compensated for the insult. The court agreed and ordered him to pay the shoemaker fifteen gulden, the equivalent of about fifty dollars. While the court's judgment pertaining to the promised marriage is unknown, Gutenberg did not marry Ennelin.

➤ THIRTY-TWO THOUSAND MIRRORS

Aachen is a city that is located 155 miles (250 kilometers) north of Strasbourg. It was the capital of Charlemagne (Charles the Great), a land named for the great ruler who founded the Holy Roman Empire in the year 800. When Charlemagne died, he was buried in Aachen Cathedral and his tomb became a shrine that housed holy relics. In 1165, the Church bestowed sainthood upon him. Beginning in the middle of the fourteenth century, every seven years the Church put the relics on display and thousands of people would make a pilgrimage to Aachen to view them.

During the pilgrimage in 1432, about ten thousand people a day had crowded into Aachen Cathedral. People believed that the relics, which supposedly included the clothing worn by Jesus at his crucifixion, had magic powers that could heal anyone who so much as looked at them. People even believed that if a mirror caught a reflection of the relics, the mirror would absorb their healing powers. Further, if a pilgrim brought that mirror home before the holiness faded, the mirror might be able to cure those too sick or weak to make the pilgrimage themselves.

In 1438, Gutenberg came up with a plan. There would be another pilgrimage to Aachen in 1439. If he got started right away, he thought he could produce thirty-two thousand mirrors that he could then sell to the pilgrims. Gutenberg had been secretly working on his printing press and he reasoned that some kind of press would be needed to make mirrors, which were made of metal in those days. Perhaps he could adapt the press he had been working on and devise a method to mass-produce mirrors.

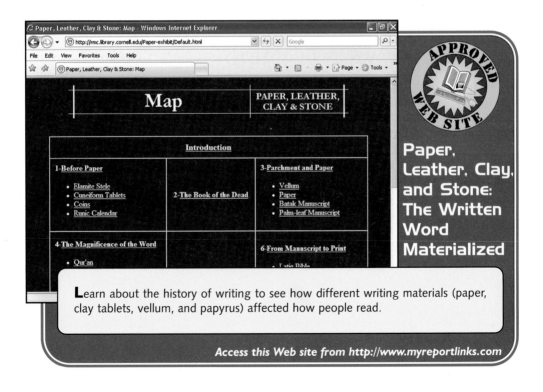

Paper, Leather, Clay, and Stone: The Written Word Materialized

Learn about the history of writing to see how different writing materials (paper, clay tablets, vellum, and papyrus) affected how people read.

Access this Web site from http://www.myreportlinks.com

John White Alexander painted this mural of Gutenberg and another man looking at a proof that was hot off the press.

and molding them into metal bars of type. The partners had barely gotten started when Andreas Dritzehn became ill. He died on December 26, 1438, a victim of the plague.

Dritzehn had two brothers who now wanted to join Gutenberg's project. When Gutenberg refused, the brothers took him to court. At the trial, Gutenberg's partners kept their promise not to reveal the true nature of the secret project. They referred to the project in vaguest terms, describing it as the "common work," the "art," and the "adventure."

A Legal Victory

After about a year, the court ruled in Gutenberg's favor. Work on the project continued. By 1440, Gutenberg had perfected the wooden printing press that used movable metal type. Historians believe that the earliest existing example of something printed with Gutenberg's movable type, a scrap of paper with eleven lines printed on each side, was printed in 1442. Regardless, with each passing year Gutenberg came closer to completing his invention. With each step toward completion, the quality of his printing steadily improved.

As spelled out in the contract, Gutenberg's business partnership ended in 1443. At the same time, Gutenberg's time in Strasbourg was quickly coming to an end. (The last bit of evidence of Gutenberg in Strasbourg is a record of his payment of an annual tax on wine dated March 12, 1444.) Gutenberg had achieved his goal, developing a printing press and a system of movable type. It was time to leave Strasbourg. But Gutenberg did not leave Strasbourg in 1444 simply because his work was finished. He left because of the threat of war.

Fleeing From the French

An army of twenty thousand French mercenaries was burning and pillaging its way north toward Strasbourg. As the mob neared Strasbourg, Gutenberg, who lived outside the city in a totally unprotected area, left. There are no records of his whereabouts for the next four years. We do not know when he returned to Mainz. The first record of his renewed presence in Mainz dates from 1448. Gutenberg's sister had died, so Gutenberg moved into his old family home.

WORKING TOWARD THE BIG BREAKTHROUGH

In 1448, the city of Mainz declared bankruptcy. The powerful guildsmen on the town council stopped the town's payment of all annuities to the patricians, meaning Gutenberg's payments stopped. Gutenberg borrowed 150 guldens from his cousin Arnold Gelthus to cover the costs of establishing a print shop. The money allowed him to set up the printing press and perfect all of the other parts of his printing process.

OVERCOMING CHALLENGES

In the course of inventing and perfecting his printing press and system of movable metal type printing, Gutenberg had to overcome many obstacles. He had to design the type, create a mold for casting the type, create the appropriate metal alloy to use to cast the mold, develop a suitable ink, and design and build the printing press.

CHAPTER

4

As difficult as each individual step in the process was, it was complicated that much further by the fact that Gutenberg had to solve each of these problems at the same time. According to writer James Moran, "Gutenberg was, therefore, forced to become a pioneer in tackling the problem of keeping one printing sub-process in step with another."[1]

In other words, if Gutenberg's system was going to work, each part of the whole had to be in place and he was responsible for designing and perfecting each of those steps. Of course, to manage the development of all the components and end with a system that worked took an inventive genius.

DESIGNING THE TYPE

Gutenberg wanted to create a style of type that would closely resemble the square, compact, handwritten letters of the scribes. Because there were no curves, the letters could easily be translated into metal. The letters of the alphabet and punctuation marks were cut in relief on the end of a steel bar called a punch. The

The development of notation (such as cuneiform and hieroglyphics), early printing processes, a reconstruction of Gutenberg's workshop, the creation of the Gutenberg Bible, and a discussion of how printing changed the world, are just some of the topics covered at **The Gutenberg Museum Mainz** Web site.

EDITOR'S CHOICE

cutting had to be carefully done with small files and scrapers. Because each page of text would have to use the same letter many times, Gutenberg made many bars for each letter of the alphabet. He made capital letters, small letters, large decorative letters called versals, and also numbers and punctuation marks.

CREATING A MOLD FOR CASTING TYPE

Some historians consider Gutenberg's design of the type mold to be his most important contribution to the evolution of printing. The typecasting process had to be incredibly precise. Each full page of text used over 1,800 characters. The depth, or thickness, of each piece of metal alloy type had to be exactly the same. So how did Gutenberg solve this problem? He created an adjustable handheld mold that could be changed to different widths. This was necessary because the width of letters varies. So the steel bars with the letters on them varied in width. A brass square, called a matrix, fit into the bottom of the adjustable mold. The punch was used to pound a sunken impression of the letter into the matrix. Molten metal was poured into the mold. When the molten metal cooled, the hinged mold was opened and the finished letter was removed. The edges of the letter were raised in relief above the base of the bar.

The finished letters were composed into words, sentences, and paragraphs. Gutenberg placed them into a frame, known as a chase, and they were locked into place to prevent them from moving during printing. The uniform and rigid printing surface of the frame, about the size of the page to be printed, was known as a form.

CREATING THE APPROPRIATE METAL ALLOY

No existing metal was suitable for Gutenberg's printing press. He needed a metal that had a low melting point, which would make it easier to produce many

identical pieces of type. Still, the metal also had to be hard enough so that it would not be damaged during printing. But metals that would be hard enough to withstand the rigors of the printing process have melting points that are too high to be practical for use in mass production of pieces of type. These requirements eliminated lead, tin, zinc, copper, and iron.

There were two metal alloys that might work: brass and bronze. But these metals, too, had problems. For example, they shrank at the moment they changed from liquid to solid. So, it would be difficult, if not impossible, to end up with a usable letter of type.

Gutenberg experimented with possibly hundreds of combinations of metals until he finally devised an appropriate alloy. It had a low melting point, making it easy to cast into type, but it was hard enough. It was economical, and it did not shrink as it cooled. Gutenberg's alloy was 80 percent lead, 15 percent antimony (a type of metal), and 5 percent tin.

DEVELOPING A SUITABLE INK

Gutenberg designed the type. He developed a method that allowed him to cast many identical letters of type. He discovered a suitable metal to use to cast those letters. After all that, he was still confronted with the problem of ink.

This statue of Johannes Gutenberg was erected in his honor in Mainz.

CROZATIER FUDIT
PARISIS MDCCCXXXVII

Gutenberg needed an ink that would stick to the metal type without running. It had to be thin enough so that it stuck to the contours of the type and printed clearly. The ink also had to stay wet long enough that it could be applied to the type and then transferred to paper before any of it dried. Finally, it could not fade much over time.

As he had in his struggle to develop a metal for casting, Gutenberg had to experiment with many different combinations of elements. After much trial and error, he discovered that using boiled linseed oil as a base, colored with lampblack, a fine soot, addressed all his needs. This ink was thick but could be easily applied to the surface of the type, but would adhere to it. The ink transferred smoothly to the surface of the paper being printed. Just as important, it dried within a reasonably short time.

DESIGNING AND BUILDING THE PRINTING PRESS

Last but definitely not least, Gutenberg needed a press that was capable of printing a large area of type. He knew of two different kinds of presses, the beam press and the screw press. Both had been invented in ancient times. The beam press was suitable for large-scale operations, like the pressing of grapes for wine or olives for olive oil.

According to James Moran:

A particular point to bear in mind is that the massive wine and paper presses were capable of great pressure, and, as such, could not possibly have been suitable to print the books for which Gutenberg and his associates, Johann Fust and Peter Schöffer, are held responsible. These books were intended to rival the best hand-produced manuscripts of the day, and a much more sensitive instrument was needed to print, for example, the magnificent pages of the forty-two-line Bible and the delicate sectional initials of the *Mainz Psalter*.[2]

Gutenberg chose the screw press, more suitable for pressing smaller quantities, as the basic

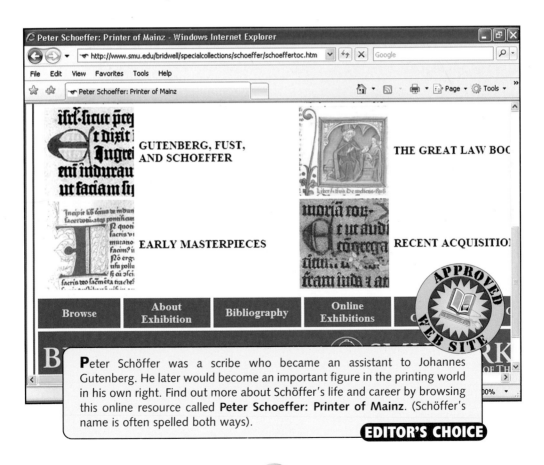

GUTENBERG, FUST, AND SCHOEFFER

THE GREAT LAW BOO

EARLY MASTERPIECES

RECENT ACQUISITIO

| Browse | About Exhibition | Bibliography | Online Exhibitions | |

Peter Schöffer was a scribe who became an assistant to Johannes Gutenberg. He later would become an important figure in the printing world in his own right. Find out more about Schöffer's life and career by browsing this online resource called **Peter Schoeffer: Printer of Mainz**. (Schöffer's name is often spelled both ways).

EDITOR'S CHOICE

Johann Fust was one of Gutenberg's business partners who aided him in the development of the printing press.

type of mechanism he would work with. But the large printing press that emerged from Gutenberg's experiments was quite different from any existing screw presses. When its wooden screws were turned, a large plate was forced down over the paper. The pressure was strong enough to force the ink from the type into the fibers of the paper. The force of the press was equal over every part of the page so that each letter printed evenly. In addition, the press was so easy to operate that the person running it would not tire quickly and slow production.

EUROPE'S FIRST BOOK PRINTED WITH MOVABLE TYPE

By 1450, Gutenberg had once again run out of money, but he was still hard at work in his shop, ready to produce his first book. Gutenberg decided that an obvious choice, one that offered a high probability of financial reward, was the *Ars Grammatica,* the standard schoolbook on Latin grammar. It was the book Gutenberg had studied when he was in school. Given Europe's much larger student population in 1450, there was already a large, built-in market for such a book.

However, Gutenberg needed more money. He found his lender in Johann Fust, a wealthy goldsmith and merchant. Fust was well-connected in Mainz. His brother Jakob was a council member, city treasurer, and future mayor. As a businessman who dealt in man-uscripts and woodblock-printed books, Fust could see the likeli-hood of substantial financial

CHAPTER

5

reward. Also, his future son-in-law Peter Schöffer was a scribe who would make a fine addition to Gutenberg's small team of assistants. So Fust loaned Gutenberg 800 gulden, equal to about $150,000 in today's money. Gutenberg's printing equipment would serve as security or collateral for the loan.

So in 1450, Gutenberg began work on *Ars Grammatica*. His plan was to make his book resemble as closely as possible those produced by scribes, but be more accurate. According to writer John Man, he did this by "preserving the unjustified right-hand margin and several variations of the same letter, incorporating the accents which scribes used to indicate short forms of words. Since this was Latin, there was no call for capital *W, X, Y* and *Z*, but what with the many variants—ten different *As,* twelve *Ps*—the type totaled 202 different characters."[1]

Within two years, Gutenberg had produced two dozen editions of *Ars Grammatica;* over the years there would be thousands of copies. Gutenberg was now ready to tackle the most ambitious project of his life—a movable-type printed version of the Bible.

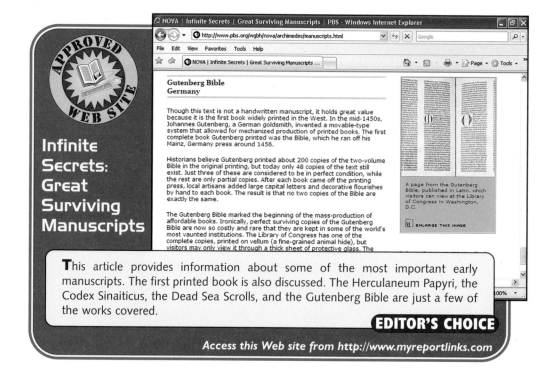

APPROVED WEB SITE

Infinite Secrets: Great Surviving Manuscripts

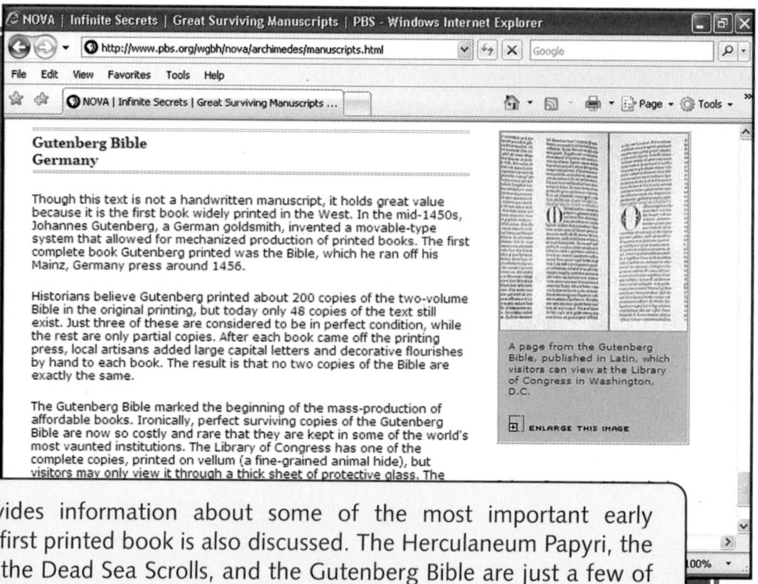
NOVA | Infinite Secrets | Great Surviving Manuscripts | PBS - Windows Internet Explorer
http://www.pbs.org/wgbh/nova/archimedes/manuscripts.html
File Edit View Favorites Tools Help
Gutenberg Bible
Germany
Though this text is not a handwritten manuscript, it holds great value because it is the first book widely printed in the West. In the mid-1450s, Johannes Gutenberg, a German goldsmith, invented a movable-type system that allowed for mechanized production of printed books. The first complete book Gutenberg printed was the Bible, which he ran off his Mainz, Germany press around 1456.
Historians believe Gutenberg printed about 200 copies of the two-volume Bible in the original printing, but today only 48 copies of the text still exist. Just three of these are considered to be in perfect condition, while the rest are only partial copies. After each book came off the printing press, local artisans added large capital letters and decorative flourishes by hand to each book. The result is that no two copies of the Bible are exactly the same.
The Gutenberg Bible marked the beginning of the mass-production of affordable books. Ironically, perfect surviving copies of the Gutenberg Bible are now so costly and rare that they are kept in some of the world's most vaunted institutions. The Library of Congress has one of the complete copies, printed on vellum (a fine-grained animal hide), but visitors may only view it through a thick sheet of protective glass. The
A page from the Gutenberg Bible, published in Latin, which visitors can view at the Library of Congress in Washington, D.C.
ENLARGE THIS IMAGE

This article provides information about some of the most important early manuscripts. The first printed book is also discussed. The Herculaneum Papyri, the Codex Sinaiticus, the Dead Sea Scrolls, and the Gutenberg Bible are just a few of the works covered.

EDITOR'S CHOICE

Access this Web site from http://www.myreportlinks.com

The Gutenberg Bible

In May 1451, Nicholas of Cusa, the German cardinal of the Roman Catholic Church, visited Mainz. He convened a meeting of seventy abbots, the priests in charge of monasteries throughout Europe. Nicholas expressed his concerns about discrepancies found in the texts of different Bibles. He knew that scribes often made mistakes when copying; he also knew that scribes occasionally made changes to the text. Nicholas was concerned that these discrepancies could one day lead to disagreements among different churches.

Enter Gutenberg, who knew that churches, monasteries, convents, and cathedrals across

Europe would be likely to purchase his Bible. Indeed, the Bible would be so expensive that only the Church and Europe's rulers could afford it.

As usual, Gutenberg was eager to begin work. And, as usual, there was one major problem: The Bible project would require a great deal of money and, once again, Gutenberg had none. Fortunately, Fust was very interested in investing and he drew up a contract. A shrewd businessman, Fust included a clause that would come to haunt Gutenberg. The clause stipulated that if Gutenberg could not repay the loan within five years,

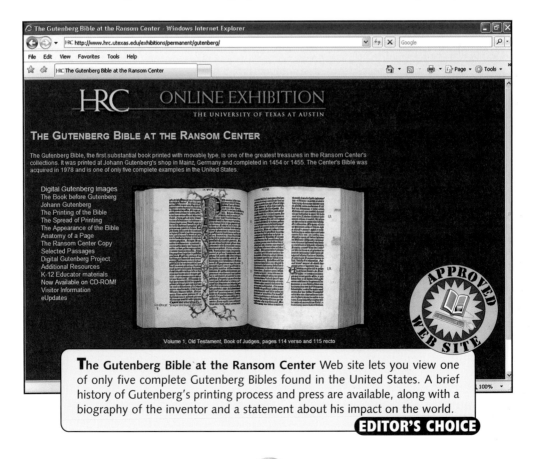

Volume 1, Old Testament, Book of Judges, pages 114 verso and 115 recto

The Gutenberg Bible at the Ransom Center Web site lets you view one of only five complete Gutenberg Bibles found in the United States. A brief history of Gutenberg's printing process and press are available, along with a biography of the inventor and a statement about his impact on the world.

EDITOR'S CHOICE

Fust would take possession of all of the equipment and inventory. This included the printing presses, the bars of type, the molds, the formulas for the ink, the paper, and printed pages.

Gutenberg was quick to agree and began work on the Bible in 1452. The *Ars Grammatica* was still being produced, as were calendars and a steady stream of very popular items known as indulgences, a document sold by the church that said that the buyer, or sinner, had confessed to his or her sins, was sorry, and had been forgiven by the church.

There were at least twenty men in Gutenberg's team of printers. Gutenberg wanted his Bible to look as if it had been hand printed by scribes, so

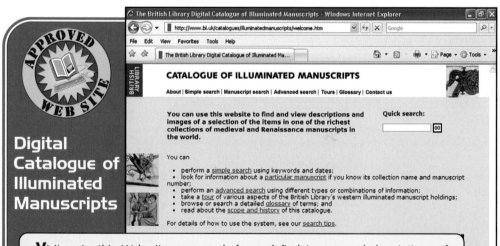

Digital Catalogue of Illuminated Manuscripts

Visitors to this Web site can search for and find images and descriptions of medieval and Renaissance illuminated manuscripts. These were beautifully illustrated handwritten books mainly produced before the invention of the printing press. Included is an online glossary of technical terms that can help the reader better understand the technology.

Access this Web site from http://www.myreportlinks.com

he had Peter Schöffer, a skilled calligrapher and illuminator, make a sample of each letter of the alphabet. Gutenberg then taught Schöffer how to make the finished type look just like his design.

→MILLION DOLLAR BIBLES

The Gutenberg Bible is known as the "forty-two-line" Bible. Each one of its 1,282 pages, bound in two volumes, contains forty-two lines of type in two columns. There are over two thousand characters on each page. The type font contains 290 different letters and symbols. Gutenberg invented the idea of justified right-hand margins, meaning the text aligned in a straight line. This was something scribes could never do. About 150 copies of the Bible, printed on paper, were produced. Thirty-nine of these, each worth millions of dollars, still exist. Approximately thirty were printed on vellum, of which twelve survive. (The skins of about five thousand calves were required to produce the vellum.)

According to John Man, Gutenberg's workshop at that time must have been an incredibly busy place. He writes:

> To print this mammoth two-volume book, with its 3 million characters, was an immense undertaking. Imagine six compositors [typesetters] and twelve printers, two to a press, positioning the typeset metal pages, laying on the ink with their fat, soft, powder-puff-shaped leather ink-balls, positioning the paper or vellum, sliding the carriage into

This engraving created by the Johnson, Fry, & Company is a depiction of Gutenberg looking over the first proof printed on his new press.

position, winding down the press, feeling for just the right amount of pressure.[2]

In 1455 about 180 copies of the Bible were nearly finished and almost ready to be sold. Considering the amount of work that went into the production of each masterpiece, Gutenberg's achievement was miraculous. Unfortunately, at what should have been the crowning triumph of his life, Gutenberg suffered a staggering setback. His partner, Fust, demanded that Gutenberg repay all the money he owed. Of course, this was impossible, primarily because all of Gutenberg's resources were tied up in the business. So Fust sued Gutenberg.

⊖ PROBLEMS WITH FUST

Some historians believe the lawsuit was a nasty plot by Fust, part of a plan to take over the business just when he knew profits would start coming in. Others think it is possible that Fust was having financial problems of his own.

If Fust was having financial problems, they were not helped any when Gutenberg decided to increase his original press run of three hundred Bibles. That decision would require going back and resetting many pages of type and delay the completion of the original three hundred copies. Perhaps Fust panicked, thinking the repayment of his loan would be delayed.

Whatever the circumstances, Gutenberg did not appear at the trial. Three men—his house servant Heinrich Keffer, Heinrich's son Bechtolf von Hanau, and the former minister of St. Christopher's Church—represented him. The court ruled that Gutenberg must immediately repay Fust the two thousand guldens he owed. Gutenberg could not, so Fust took possession of the printing presses, all of the printing equipment, (including the metal type) and, most significantly, all of the Bibles. Suddenly, Fust was in control of all of the products of Gutenberg's inventive genius.

Fust Opens Shop

Fust set up his own printing shop, taking his son-in-law Peter Schöffer as a partner. He also hired other printers from Gutenberg's workshop and completed Gutenberg's Bibles. He sold them for a handsome profit. Gutenberg earned nothing from their sale.

The Gutenberg Bible is a marvel of technology and art. According to Albert Kapr, an expert on the subject:

> It still appears miraculous that this first typographic book in Europe . . . should be of such sublime beauty and mastery that later generations up to our own day have rarely matched and never excelled in quality. For regularity of setting, uniform silky blackness of impression, harmony of layout, and many other respects, it is magisterial in

a way to which we can rarely aspire under modern conditions. Behind such an achievement can only have stood a personality inspired by a passionate commitment to excellence, and able to communicate this drive and enthusiasm to his fellow workers.[3]

→ GUTENBERG'S FINAL YEARS

Sadly, after the trial in 1455, Gutenberg was once again left with nothing. He did however, have the friendship of Konrad Humery, the town clerk of Mainz, who loaned him money for a printing press and some type. By 1457, Gutenberg was back in business.

That same year, the Fust-Schöffer printshop published the *Mainz Psalter*. It was a collection of psalms, songs of praise, prayers, extracts from the Old and New Testaments, religious poems, and other religious items. Like the Bibles he won in the court decision, this major work had been begun by Gutenberg. Unfortunately, Gutenberg had never printed his name on any of his work, leading to quite a bit of confusion for historians. This also made it possible for Fust and Schöffer not only to claim credit for the *Mainz Psalter* but for inventing the process used to print it. This was the first book to include a printer's imprint, which appeared on the first page:

The present copy of the Psalms, adorned with venerable capital letters and also distinguished by

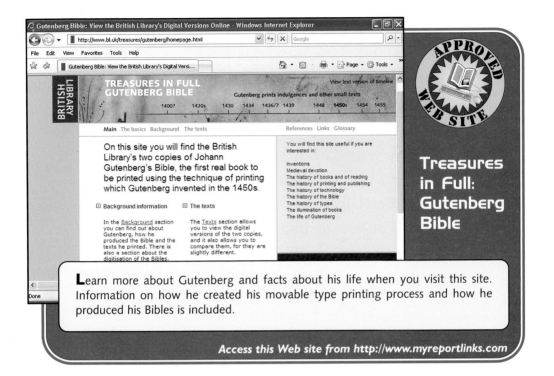

TREASURES IN FULL
GUTENBERG BIBLE

On this site you will find the British Library's two copies of Johann Gutenberg's Bible, the first real book to be printed using the technique of printing which Gutenberg invented in the 1450s.

Treasures in Full: Gutenberg Bible

Learn more about Gutenberg and facts about his life when you visit this site. Information on how he created his movable type printing process and how he produced his Bibles is included.

Access this Web site from http://www.myreportlinks.com

appropriate rubrications, was so fashioned thanks to the ingenious discovery of imprinting and forming letters without any use of a pen and completed with diligence to the glory of God by Johann Fust, citizen of Mainz, and Peter Schöffer of Gernsheim, in the year of our Lord 1457, on the Vigil [eve] of the Assumption [of the Virgin Mary] [i.e. 14 August].[4]

Fust and Schöffer went on to enjoy tremendous success, producing one religious work after another. The party for Fust ended in 1466. While on a sales trip to Paris, he caught the plague and died. Schöffer, who had married Fust's daughter, inherited the printing business and continued to have great success.

GUTENBERG STARTS OVER

Meanwhile, Gutenberg was once again hard at work in his newly equipped print shop. He designed and cast new type. He printed more copies of his Latin grammar book, as well as calendars. There is also evidence that in 1459 he became involved in a cooperative project with a new print shop in the city of Bamberg.

The bishop of Bamberg, Georg von Schaumburg, wanted a Bible of his own, but the forty-two-line Bibles had all been sold. So the bishop had his secretary, Albrecht Pfister, set up a print shop and produce a Bible. Gutenberg sent his own type and a few of his printers to Bamberg to help. Then Gutenberg did some of the work on the new thirty-six-line Bible.

Around this time, Gutenberg turned his attention to still another major project, the *Catholicon,* a Latin encyclopedia. The book, compiled by a friar named Giovanni Balbi in the mid-1200s, was sort of a combined dictionary and book of grammar. The original version consisted of fifteen hundred pages. Gutenberg's printed version, which appeared in 1460, was set in very small type, had 746 pages, and contained an amazing 5 million characters.

At the end of the *Catholicon* are the only words we actually know that Gutenberg wrote. He dedicated the work to God "at whose bidding the tongues of infants become eloquent, and who

Nikolaus Karl Eduard Schmidt von der Launitz created this sculpture of Johannes Gutenberg, Johann Fust, and Peter Schöffer to commemorate the invention of the printing press. The sculpture resides in Hamburg, Germany.

often reveals to the lowly what he conceals from the wise." The dedication also boasts about its origins in glorious Mainz in "the year of our Lord's incarnation 1460," and makes much of its production "without help of reed, stylus, or quill, but by a wonderful concord, proportion and measure of punches and formes."[5]

In 1462, the political situation in Mainz suddenly took a turn for the worse. The town was caught in the middle of a power struggle between two rival archbishops of the Roman Catholic Church. Dieter von Isenberg and Adolf von Nassau,

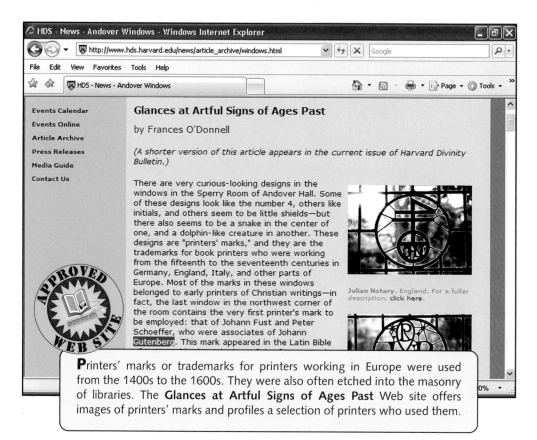

Printers' marks or trademarks for printers working in Europe were used from the 1400s to the 1600s. They were also often etched into the masonry of libraries. The **Glances at Artful Signs of Ages Past** Web site offers images of printers' marks and profiles a selection of printers who used them.

This image is of a page of a Gutenberg Bible.

who had the backing of the pope, were at odds. Most of the townspeople favored von Isenberg, who challenged the power of the Church to tax them. Von Nassau's five-hundred-man army sacked the town, killing more than four hundred people. Most of the citizens fled, including Gutenberg, who once again went to Eltville where he set up another print shop.

Gutenberg remained in Eltville until von Nassau invited him back to Mainz in January 1465. Von Nassau offered Gutenberg a complete pardon, saying "We have recognized the agreeable and willing service which our dear, faithful Johannes Gutenberg has rendered, and may and shall

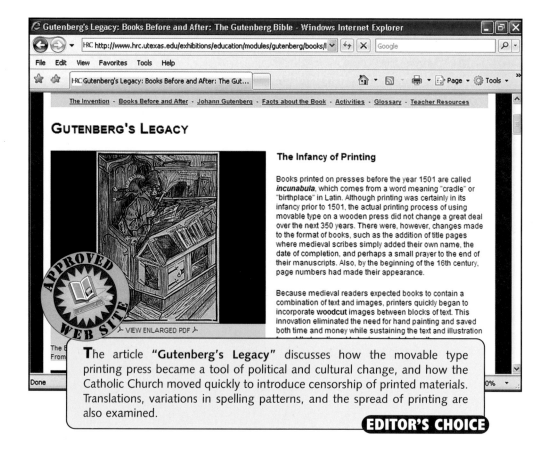

The Invention · Books Before and After · Johann Gutenberg · Facts about the Book · Activities · Glossary · Teacher Resources

GUTENBERG'S LEGACY

The Infancy of Printing

Books printed on presses before the year 1501 are called *incunabula*, which comes from a word meaning "cradle" or "birthplace" in Latin. Although printing was certainly in its infancy prior to 1501, the actual printing process of using movable type on a wooden press did not change a great deal over the next 350 years. There were, however, changes made to the format of books, such as the addition of title pages where medieval scribes simply added their own name, the date of completion, and perhaps a small prayer to the end of their manuscripts. Also, by the beginning of the 16th century, page numbers had made their appearance.

Because medieval readers expected books to contain a combination of text and images, printers quickly began to incorporate woodcut images between blocks of text. This innovation eliminated the need for hand painting and saved both time and money while sustaining the text and illustration

VIEW ENLARGED PDF

The article **"Gutenberg's Legacy"** discusses how the movable type printing press became a tool of political and cultural change, and how the Catholic Church moved quickly to introduce censorship of printed materials. Translations, variations in spelling patterns, and the spread of printing are also examined.

EDITOR'S CHOICE

render in the future . . . We shall, each and every year, when we clothe our ordinary courtiers, clothe him at the same time like one of our noblemen."[6]

In honor of his achievements and to make up for past wrongs, Gutenberg was granted the honorary title of "Hofmann" (Gentleman of the Court). Gutenberg was also promised an annual pension and 2,000 kilograms (about 4,409 lbs.) of grain and 2,000 liters (about 520 gallons) of wine, tax free.

Gutenberg died three years later, on February 3, 1468. He was buried in Mainz at the Convent of the Barefoot Friars in an unmarked grave. An inscription in a book printed in 1470 with the new technology, probably scribbled by Leonhard Mengoss, Eltville's priest, says, "A.D. 1468, on St Blasius' Day [3 February] died the honored master Henne Ginsfleiss [for Gutenberg was also known as Gensfleisch, and still is in Eltville] on whom God have mercy."[7] This is the only evidence we have of the date of the great inventor's death.

In 1505, thirty-seven years after Gutenberg's death, Johann Schoeffer, the grandson of Johann Fust and son of Peter Schöffer, paid tribute to Gutenberg. In the dedication to a book, Schoeffer wrote that the book was printed in Mainz, the city where Johannes Gutenberg had invented the art of typography in 1450.

HOW GUTENBERG'S MOVABLE TYPE CHANGED THE WORLD

Johannes Gutenberg was a brilliant inventor, an ambitious businessman, a talented manager of men and materials, and an expert craftsman. Yet for all of these abilities, he was never financially successful. He constantly ran out of money, having to borrow from friends, relatives, and business associates. He was involved in numerous court battles, some of which he won, others he lost. But despite these challenges and other obstacles, he still managed to give the world the printing press and a system of movable metal type, a contribution that changed the world.

➔ THE PRINTING EXPLOSION IN EUROPE

By the time of Gutenberg's death in 1468, his invention was quickly spreading across Europe. In 1464 two Germans set up a press in Rome; in or before 1469 two Germans opened a printing shop in Venice; in 1470 three Germans brought the art to

CHAPTER

6

Paris; in 1471 it reached Holland, in 1472 Switzerland, in 1473 Hungary, in 1474 Spain, in 1476 England, in 1482 Denmark, in 1483 Sweden, in 1490 Constantinople."[1]

As a direct result of the printing press, news and information began to travel much faster than it ever had and books became more readily available to everyone, not just the wealthy. Printed news sheets, sold cheaply, gave people the latest information on European and world events. One such sheet, printed in 1493, described the voyage of Christopher Columbus to the New World.

In 1470, Guillaume Fichet of Paris raved about the invention of printing in a letter. He wrote, "There has been discovered in Germany a wonderful new method for the production of books, and those who have mastered the art are taking it from Mainz out into the world. . . . The light of this discovery will spread from Germany to all parts of the earth."[2]

By 1499, printing shops had become established in more than 250 cities around Europe. An estimated 8 million to perhaps as many as 15 million books, including 30,000 different titles, had been printed by movable-type printing presses. "A man born in 1453, the year of the fall of Constantinople, could look back from his fiftieth year on a lifetime in which about 8 million books had been printed, more perhaps than all the scribes of Europe had produced since Constantine founded his city in A.D. 330."[3] More people were reading than ever before, and a passion for books became the hallmark of the age.

Not everybody was happy about the development of the printing press. As the printed word swept Europe, scribes were faced with rising unemployment. Wealthy nobles feared that printing

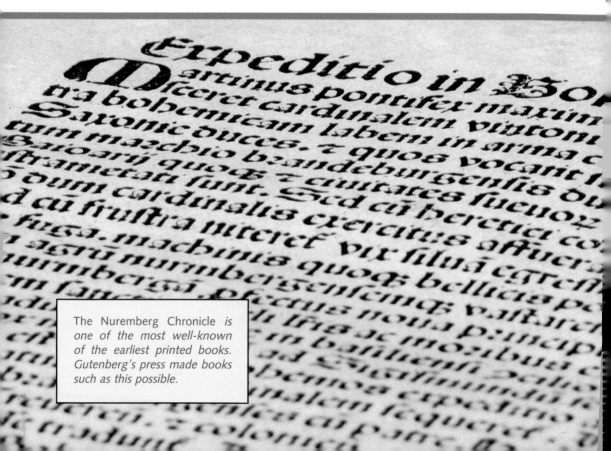

The Nuremberg Chronicle *is one of the most well-known of the earliest printed books. Gutenberg's press made books such as this possible.*

would lower the value of their manuscript libraries. Some statesmen and clergy distrusted printing as a possible means of spreading subversive ideas.

Competition between scribes and printers continued for decades.

> More than fifty years after the publication of the book we call the Gutenberg Bible, the issue was still alive even in Gutenberg's own country, where printers were more numerous than they were anywhere else in the world. In 1494, a quarter century after Gutenberg's death, the Abbot of Sponheim—a German cleric, whose interests included not only copying but also shorthand, cryptography, and the possibility that angels might be employed to carry secret messages over long distances—wrote a treatise called De Laude Scriptorum ("In Praise of Scribes"), in which he argued that monks should not allow the invention of printing to stop them from copying books by hand. He contended that handwritten books would last longer than printed ones, and that hand copying itself was a virtuous activity because a copyist could pause in the course of his work to pray. To ensure that his treatise received the readership it deserved, the Abbot had it printed.[4]

⮡ THE SPREAD OF IDEAS

The Renaissance took root in the growing city-states of northern Italy early in the fourteenth century without the benefit of printing. The times were marked by an increase in trade and travel.

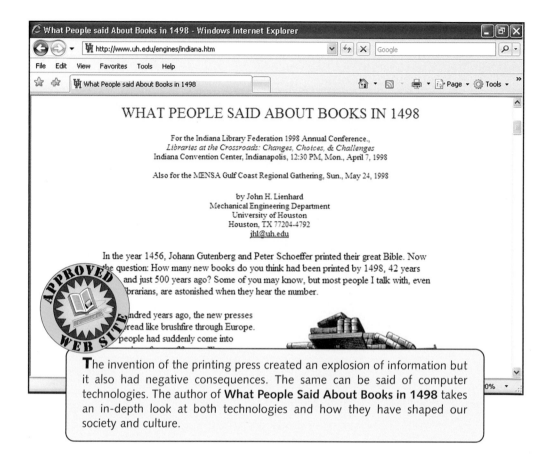

WHAT PEOPLE SAID ABOUT BOOKS IN 1498

For the Indiana Library Federation 1998 Annual Conference.,
Libraries at the Crossroads: Changes, Choices, & Challenges
Indiana Convention Center, Indianapolis, 12:30 PM, Mon., April 7, 1998

Also for the MENSA Gulf Coast Regional Gathering, Sun., May 24, 1998

by John H. Lienhard
Mechanical Engineering Department
University of Houston
Houston, TX 77204-4792
jhl@uh.edu

In the year 1456, Johann Gutenberg and Peter Schoeffer printed their great Bible. Now the question: How many new books do you think had been printed by 1498, 42 years and just 500 years ago? Some of you may know, but most people I talk with, even librarians, are astonished when they hear the number.

...ndred years ago, the new presses ...read like brushfire through Europe. ...people had suddenly come into

The invention of the printing press created an explosion of information but it also had negative consequences. The same can be said of computer technologies. The author of **What People Said About Books in 1498** takes an in-depth look at both technologies and how they have shaped our society and culture.

Renaissance scholars studied ancient Latin manuscripts which had been preserved in monasteries. Then, when Constantinople fell to the Ottoman Turks in 1453, Byzantine scholars fled to Rome with ancient Greek manuscripts. Renaissance artists and thinkers studied the works of classical culture. They developed a new outlook on life known as humanism, a focus on human potential and achievements.

The birth and development of the printing press helped spread the ideas of the Renaissance to northern Europe. At first, printers produced mainly religious works. Soon they began to provide books on other subjects, such as travel guides, books of etiquette, medical and diet manuals, and accounts of the great voyages of discovery. The availability of books encouraged people to learn to read, which led to a dramatic rise in literacy. Printing was also a huge benefit to science. Printed texts were so consistent that scientists in different countries could work with one another by reference to specific pages of specific editions of books or articles. Printing was a major reason why science advanced dramatically in the following centuries.

Gutenberg to Gates: Five Hundred Years of Books From Printing Press to Computer

Using rare books from the Springfield Library Special Collections, this online exhibit begins with the birth of printing and ends with a discussion of the future of books. A short time line of the history of books and printing is included.

Access this Web site from http://www.myreportlinks.com

During the Middle Ages, all learning and education was controlled by the Roman Catholic Church. All books were written in Latin. As the printing revolution spread throughout Europe, books were initially published in Latin. But before long, books, including the Bible, became available in the languages that were more commonly used by the majority of Europeans—German, English, French, Italian, and Spanish. As a direct result, many people who could not afford a classical education that would teach them Latin could now buy books they could read.

One immediate result of this achievement of printing was the appearance of an abundance of Bibles in the

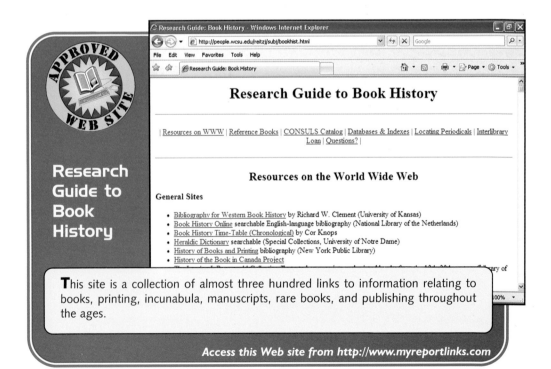

Research Guide to Book History

This site is a collection of almost three hundred links to information relating to books, printing, incunabula, manuscripts, rare books, and publishing throughout the ages.

Access this Web site from http://www.myreportlinks.com

world. Another was a cheapening of schoolbooks. The knowledge of reading spread swiftly. There was not only a great increase of books in the world, but the books that were now made were plainer to read and so easier to understand. Instead of toiling at a crabbed text and then thinking over its significance, readers now could think unimpeded as they read. With this increase in the facility of reading, the reading public grew. The book ceased to be a highly decorated toy or a scholar's mystery. People began to write books to be read as well as looked at by ordinary people.[5]

Once people were able to read the Bible in their own language, they no longer had to rely on priests to interpret it for them. People became more critical of priests and their behavior. This eventually led to demands for religious reform.

⇒ THE PROTESTANT REFORMATION

When Martin Luther tacked his essay onto the door of the Castle Church in Wittenburg on October 31, 1517, he had no way of knowing that he was helping ignite what would come to be known as the Protestant Reformation. But neither did he know that someone would copy his 95 Theses or that they would soon be read, considered, and debated all over Europe. But that essay was just the start. During the following years, the German monk and scholar continued to attack the Church, his fiery writing and inflammatory ideas continuing to reach a wide audience all over Europe. Indeed, Luther's writing and the wide audience they received thanks to Gutenberg's printing press brought about just the sort of changes that religious and political leaders had feared just a few decades earlier.[6]

Martin Luther understood and appreciated the importance of Gutenberg's invention and the role it played in changing the world. He saw the printing press as a blessing from God that would free the German nation from the control of the pope in Rome.

"Between 1517 and 1520, Luther's thirty publications probably sold well over 300,000 copies . . . Altogether in relation to the spread of religious ideas it seems difficult to exaggerate the significance of the

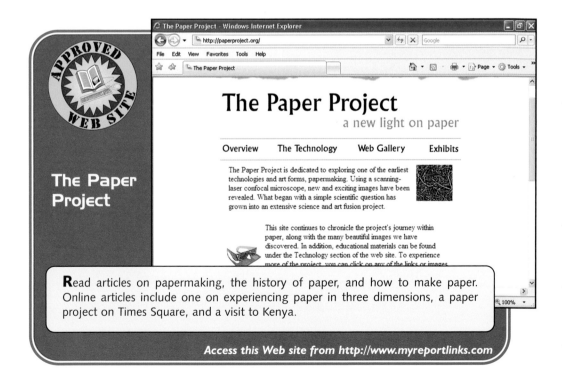

The Paper Project

Read articles on papermaking, the history of paper, and how to make paper. Online articles include one on experiencing paper in three dimensions, a paper project on Times Square, and a visit to Kenya.

Access this Web site from http://www.myreportlinks.com

Press, without which a revolution of this magnitude could scarcely have been consummated."[7]

In 1542, the German historian Johann Sleidan, in *An Address to the Estates of the Empire,* commented on the profound influence of printing:

> As if to offer proof that God has chosen us to accomplish a special mission, there was invented in our land a marvelous new and subtle art, the art of printing. This opened German eyes even as it is now bringing enlightenment to other countries. Each man became eager for knowledge, not without feeling a sense of amazement at his former blindness.[8]

ADVANCES IN PRINTING

Since the 1500s there have been many advancements in the field of printing. With each new invention, it seems that people have been able to receive information more quickly and easily. The printed word has helped inform and unite people ever since. For example, the printing press allowed writer Thomas Paine to distribute his book *Common Sense.* Many of the people who read the book began to believe in the cause of the American Patriots, which led to the Revolutionary War.

Samuel Morse sent the first telegraph in 1836. Morse used a machine to type out a series of clicks which were then sent along a copper telegraph wire. Someone at the other end of the wire would receive the message and translate the clicks into

Printing has come a long way since Gutenberg's invention. This is an image of a modern print shop.

letters. Now a person could send a message to someone hundreds of miles away quickly and fairly easily.

In 1865, a printer named William Bullock developed a system of offset printing which allowed people to print on both sides of a sheet of paper at once. By doing this, he was able to print newspapers very quickly. Now a newspaper could easily print more than one edition in a day. That way, if something important happened after the morning edition was printed, that news item could be added to the evening edition.

⊜ PRINTING AND INSTANT COMMUNICATION

By 1876, with Alexander Graham Bell's invention of the telephone, it was possible to communicate with someone instantly without having to send a letter or a printed page. Bell was able to send and receive sound and speech over wires much like the wires Morse used to send his telegraph messages. Sending sound over wires eventually led to the ability to send all sorts of data through telephone lines.

Of course, there was still a need to print information. People wanted to read, books, letters, newspapers and other items. Still, many people wanted to print their own information rather than writing it out. In 1873, Charles Latham Sholes perfected the typewriter and it became available soon after. Now, a person could type up their own pamphlet or their own letters and send them to whomever they wished. Or, they could submit them to newspapers or publishers so their thoughts could be distributed over a wide area.

Another major breakthrough was the creation of the first computer that was available for purchase. The UNIVAC, as it was called, was nothing like the computers that people have in their homes today. It was a huge machine with a main processing unit that was the size of a large refrigerator. Still, the UNIVAC could perform operations and then instantly spew out data onto punch cards that could be read and analyzed. Computers would continue to develop, becoming smaller, faster, and more affordable. In 1977, Apple Computer sold a personal computer that many people could afford to have in their homes for the first time. This was the point at which computers started to resemble what we have in our homes today.

COMPUTERS AND PRINTING

Computers are continually improving the way in which companies publish books and magazines. As recently as the late 1980s, printing presses still used metal plates, somewhat like Gutenberg had used, to print their books. Now everything is done digitally. Book and magazine publishers send printing presses digital files that are simply loaded

Lucas sirus·natione anthiocensis·arte medicus·discipulus apostolorum·postea paulum secutus usque ad confessionem eius seruiens domino sine crimine: nam neque uxorem unquam habuit neque filios:septuaginta et quatuor annorum obijt in bithinia·plenus spiritu sancto. Qui cum iam scripta essent euangelia·per matheum quidem in iudea·per marcum autem in italia:sancto instigante spiritu in achaie partibus hoc scripsit euangelium:significans etiam ipse in principio ante suum alia esse descripta. Cui extra ea quae ordo euangelice dispositionis exposita maxime necessitas laboris fuit:ut primum grecis fidelibus omni perfectatione uenturi in carne dei cristi manifestata humanitate ne iudaicis fabulis attenti: in solo legis desiderio tenerentur: uel ne hereticis fabulis et stultis solicitationibus seducti exciderent a ueritate elaboraret:dehinc ut in principio euangelij iohannis natiuitate presumpta·cui euangelium scriberet et in quo electus scriberet indicaret: contestans in se completa esse quae essent ab alijs inchoata. Cui ideo post baptismum filij dei a perfectione generationis in cristo implere reprendit a principio natiuitatis humane potestas permissa est: ut requirentibus demonstraret in quo apprehendes erat pre nathan filium dauid introitu recurrentis in deum generationis admisso indisparabilis dei predicans in hominibus cristum suum·perfecti opus hois redire in se per filium faceret:qui per dauid patrem uenientibus iter prebebat in cristo. Cui luce non immerito etiam scribendorum actuum apostolorum potestas in ministerio datur:ut deo in deum pleno et filio perditionis extincto·oratione ab apostolis

facta·sorte domini electionis numerus compleretur: sicque paulus consummatione apostolicis actibus daretur·quem diu contra stimulum recalcitrante dominus elegisset. Quod et legentibus ac requirentibus deum·et si per singula expediri a nobis utile fuerat:sciens tamen quod operantem agricolam oportet de suis fructibus edere·uitauimus publicam curiositatem:ne non tam uolentibus deum demonstrare uideremur·quam fastidientibus prodidisse. Explicit prefatio. Incipit euangelium secundum lucam. Prologus [...] [...] luce in euangelium suum [...]

Quoniam quidem multi conati sunt ordinare narrationes quae in nobis complete sunt rerum·sicut tradiderunt nobis qui ab initio ipsi uiderunt·et ministri fuerunt sermonis:uisum est et michi assecuto omnia a principio diligenter ex ordine tibi scribere optime theophile : ut cognoscas eorum uerborum de quibus eruditus es ueritatem.

Fuit in diebus herodis regis iudee sacerdos quidam nomine zacharias de uice abia·et uxor illi de filiabus aaron : et nomen eius elizabeth. Erant autem iusti ambo ante deum: incedentes in omnibus mandatis et iustificationibus domini sine querela. Et non erat illis filius·eo quod esset elizabeth sterilis : et ambo processissent in diebus suis. Factum est autem cum sacerdotio fungeretur zacharias in ordine uicis sue ante deum: secundum consuetudinem sacerdotij sorte exijt ut incensum poneret ingressus in templum domini. Et omnis multitudo populi erat orans foris hora incensi. Apparuit autem illi angelus domini : stans a dextris altaris incensi. Et zacharias turbatus est videns : et timor irruit sup eu. Ait aut ad illu agelus. Ne timeas zacharia: quonia exaudita est depratio tua. Et uxor tua elizabeth pariet tibi filiu · et vocabis nomen eius iohannem:et erit gaudium tibi et exultatio:et multi in natiuitate eius gaudebut. Erit enim magnus corā dno : et vinu et siceram nō bibet. Et spiritu sancto replebitur adhuc ex utero matris sue : z multos filiorū istl' couertet ad dnm deum ipsoy. Et ipe precedet ante ipm i spiritu et virtute helie:ut conuertat corda patru in filios·et incredibiles ad prudentiā iustoy:parare dno plebe pfectā. Et dixit zacharias ad angelu. Unde hoc scia? Ego enī sum senex:et uxor mea pcessit in diebz suis. Et respodens angelus dixit ei. Ego sum gabriel q asto ante deum:z missus sum loqui ad te:z hec tibi euangelizare. Et ecce eris tacens et non poteris loqui usqz i diem quo hec fiant : pro eo op non credidisti verbis meis·que implebutur in tempore suo. Et erat plebs expectans zachariā: et mirabātur op tardaret ipe i templo. Egressus aut non poterat loqui ad illos. Et cognouerut op visionem vidisset i templo. Et ipe erat innuens illis: et pmansit mutus. Et factu est ut impleti sunt dies officii eiº:abijt i domu suā. Post hos aut dies cocepit elizabeth uxor eius:z occultabat se mesibz quinqz dicens. Quia sic fecit michi dominus·in diebus quibus respexit auferre obprobriu meu inter homines. In mense aut sexto missus e angelus gabriel a deo in ciuitatem galilee cui nomen nazareth·ad uirginem desposatam viro cui nomē erat ioseph · de domo damid:et nomē uirginis maria.

Et ingressus āgelus ad eā dixit. Aue gratia plena:dns tecu:benedicta tu in mulieribz.Que cu audisset-turbata est in sermone eius : et cogitabat qualis esset ista salutatio. Et ait angelus ei. Ne timeas maria : inuenisti eni gratiam apud deū. Ecce concipies in utero et paries filiu:z vocabis nomen eius ihesum.Hic erit magnus : z filiº altissimi vocabitur. Et dabit illi dns deº sedem dauid patris eius : et regnabit i domo iacob in eternu : et regni eiº nō erit finis. Dixit aut maria ad angelū. Quomō fiet istud : quonia viru non cognosco? Et respodens angelus dixit ei. Spiritus sanctus superueniet in te:z virtus altissimi obumbrabit tibi. Ideoqz et qd nascef ex te sanctu : vocabit filiº dei. Et ecce elizabeth cognata tua:z ipa cocepit filiu i senectute sua. Et hic mesis est sextº illi q uocat sterilis? Quia nō erit impossibile apud deum omne verbū. Dixit aut maria. Ecce ancilla dni:fiat michi secundū verbū tuū. Et discessit ab illa āgelus. Exurgens aut maria in diebus illis abijt in motana cu festinatione in ciuitate iuda:et intrauit in domū zacharie:z salutauit elizabeth. Et factu est ut audiuit salutationem marie elizabeth:exultauit infans in utero eiº. Et repleta est spiritu sancto elizabeth : et exclamauit voce magna z dixit. Benedicta tu inter mulieres:z benedictus fructus uentris tui. Et unde hoc michi:ut veniat mater dni mei ad me? Ecce enim ut facta est vox salutationis tue i auribz meis : exultauit in gaudio infans in utero meo. Et beata que credidit:quonia pficientur ea q dicta sunt ei a dno. Et ait maria. Magnificat anima mea dnm: et exultauit spiritus meus in

into a computer and printed onto films that are copied over and over again before the books are bound. In some cases, writers and companies publish books without even printing them, selling e-books over the Internet.

Perhaps the most important invention of the last twenty years has been the use of the Internet. Started as a U.S. government project, use of the Internet was released to the public in 1994. Tim Berners-Lee is the one most often credited with the development of the World Wide Web. This is the part of the Internet that most of us use when

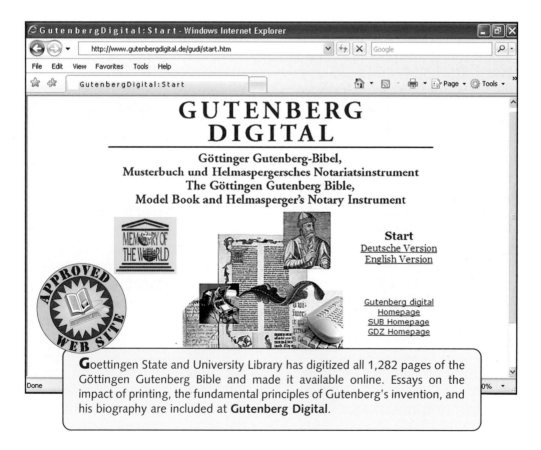

Goettingen State and University Library has digitized all 1,282 pages of the Göttingen Gutenberg Bible and made it available online. Essays on the impact of printing, the fundamental principles of Gutenberg's invention, and his biography are included at **Gutenberg Digital**.

we visit our favorite Web sites. Because of the Web, people all over the world can send messages, images, movies, and other things to one another in an instant. It is also very easy for someone to create their own Web page, allowing them to publish their thoughts in a way that anyone else with an Internet connection can view and read them.

Today it is easy for us to take printing and all the forms of mass communication that evolved from it for granted. Sending e-mails, text messaging, printing documents from our personal computers, and instant messaging have become routine parts of many of our lives. But stop for a moment and consider what our world might be like had Gutenberg not invented the printing press—it would be very different indeed, one where even a book like the one you are holding in your hand might be available to just a fortunate few. We all owe a huge debt to Johannes Gutenberg, the printer who gave words to the world.

PRINTING EXPERIMENTS

Printing from woodblocks and Gutenberg's invention of printing using movable metal type are very similar techniques. Both are a form of relief printing. In other words, in each method of printing, the ink is applied to surfaces that stand out in relief, or stick out, from a background that is not inked. When paper is pressed onto those surfaces and then pulled away, much of the ink comes with it, producing the image on the paper.

To demonstrate how this principle works, try the following block printing experiments.

Activities 1 and 2: Block Printing with Cardboard Blocks

⮎ MATERIALS:
- **Pen or pencil**
- **Scissors**
- **Thin cardboard**
- **Glue**
- **Glue brush**

A Heavenly Craft: The Woodcut in Early Printed Books (A Library of Congress Exhibition) - Windows Internet Expl...

http://www.loc.gov/exhibits/heavenlycraft/

Google

File   Edit   View   Favorites   Tools   Help

Heavenly Craft: The Woodcut in Early Printed Books (...

Page   Tools

The Library of Congress >> Exhibitions   Find   in Heavenly Craft Exhibit Pages   GO

A HEAVENLY CRAFT
THE WOODCUT IN EARLY PRINTED BOOKS

A Heavenly Craft: The Woodcut in Early Printed Books is a Library of Congress exhibition that presents for the first time all the woodcut-illustrated books purchased by Lessing J. Rosenwald at the Dyson Perrins sale, now part of the legendary Rosenwald Collection at the Library of Congress. These books were printed within the first century after Gutenberg mastered the art of printing with moveable type.

- Overview
- Introduction
- 15th Century
- 16th Century
- Checklist of Objects
- Learn More About It
- Acknowledgments
- Read News Release

The physical exhibition is no longer o

APPROVED WEB SITE

Saint Birgitta. *Revelationes*. Nuremberg
September 21, 1500. Rosenwald Collec
Special Collections Division, Library of Co

The online exhibition **A Heavenly Craft: The Woodcut in Early Printed Books** takes a look at the development of the woodcut, an artistic technique in printmaking. The Web site explores the evolution of woodcutting using examples from French, Spanish, Italian, and German printers.

- **Plastic tray**
- **Printing inks**
- **Paper clips**
- **Printing sheet**
- **Roller**
- **Paper**

 **OVERPRINTING**

- Draw a design on a sheet of paper.

- Cut out the shapes of the design.

- Glue the shapes onto a sheet of cardboard.

- Allow them to dry.

- Place a sheet of paper over the design on the cardboard.

- Attach the paper to the cardboard with paper clips to hold it steady.

- Coat the roller with ink and roll it carefully over the paper.

The design on the cardboard block will slowly appear.

PRINTING WITH THE INKED BLOCK

- Apply the ink to the cardboard block evenly with the roller.

- Lay the block face down onto a sheet of paper.

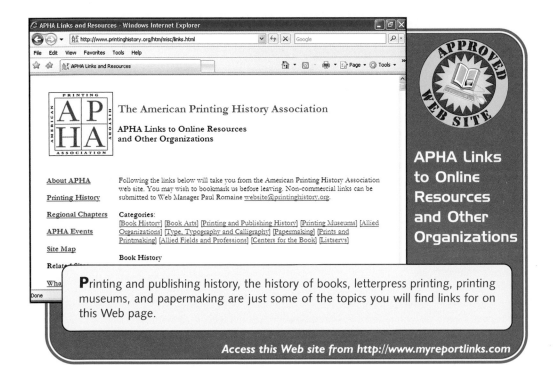

The American Printing History Association

APHA Links to Online Resources and Other Organizations

About APHA

Printing History

Regional Chapters

APHA Events

Site Map

Following the links below will take you from the American Printing History Association web site. You may wish to bookmark us before leaving. Non-commercial links can be submitted to Web Manager Paul Romaine website@printinghistory.org.

Categories:
[Book History] [Book Arts] [Printing and Publishing History] [Printing Museums] [Allied Organizations] [Type, Typography and Calligraphy] [Papermaking] [Prints and Printmaking] [Allied Fields and Professions] [Centers for the Book] [Listservs]

Book History

APHA Links to Online Resources and Other Organizations

Printing and publishing history, the history of books, letterpress printing, printing museums, and papermaking are just some of the topics you will find links for on this Web page.

Access this Web site from http://www.myreportlinks.com

• Press the block gently, to make sure a good print is transferred to the paper.

• Lift the block carefully to reveal the print.

You can try block printing experiments using a variety of other materials to make the block. Instead of cardboard, try using clay or a household sponge—you can even use a raw potato!

Report Links

The Internet sites described below can be accessed at
http://www.myreportlinks.com

▶**The Gutenberg Bible at the Ransom Center**
Editor's Choice The University of Texas' online exhibition of the Gutenberg Bible.

▶**The Gutenberg Museum Mainz**
Editor's Choice Visit one of the world's oldest printing museums.

▶**Infinite Secrets: Great Surviving Manuscripts**
Editor's Choice PBS presents this short history of old manuscripts.

▶**"Gutenberg's Legacy"**
Editor's Choice A look at changes that came about when Gutenberg's press was invented.

▶**From Manuscript to Print: The Evolution of the Medieval Book**
Editor's Choice This Cornell University Library's site celebrates the evolution of writing.

▶**Peter Schoeffer: Printer of Mainz**
Editor's Choice An online lecture celebrating the creative genius of Peter Schöffer.

▶**APHA Links to Online Resources and Other Organizations**
The American Printing History Association has some good links on the subject.

▶**China's Gifts to the West**
A great overview of Chinese inventions and contributions to the world.

▶***Diamond Sutra***
The British Library offers a presentation of landmarks in the craft of printing.

▶**The *Diamond Sutra***
You can read a translation of the *Diamond Sutra* when you visit this site.

▶**Digital Catalogue of Illuminated Manuscripts**
This searchable database is a digitized catalogue of illustrated manuscripts.

▶**Glances at Artful Signs of Ages Past**
Learn something about printers' marks from this Web site.

▶**Gutenberg Bible Goes Digital**
Read a National Public Radio presentation on digitizing the Gutenberg Bible.

▶**Gutenberg Digital**
This bilingual site (German and English) has a full version of a digitized Gutenberg Bible.

▶**The Gutenberg Galaxy Revisited: Print, Drama, and the English Reformation**
Bowdoin College has an article on how printing helped bring about the Protestant Reformation.

Report Links

The Internet sites described below can be accessed at http://www.myreportlinks.com

▶**Gutenberg to Gates: Five Hundred Years of Books From Printing Press to Computer**
This site explores the development of the book after the invention of movable type printing.

▶**A Heavenly Craft: The Woodcut in Early Printed Books**
The Library of Congress examines books after Gutenberg mastered the art of printing.

▶**History of Paper**
Watch a video of a woman in Japan making paper.

▶**Incunabula: Dawn of Western Printing**
For a good overview on incunabula, browse this Web site.

▶**Invention Dimension**
MIT offers this savvy resource on famous inventors and their inventions.

▶**Paper and Watermark Museum of Fabriano**
Visit one of the more important paper museums in the world.

▶**Paper, Leather, Clay, and Stone: The Written Word Materialized**
Cornell University Library traces words from stone tablets to modern printing.

▶**Paper Online**
This is a nice overview of how paper is produced.

▶**The Paper Project**
Learn about papermaking when you visit this Web site.

▶**Pre-Gutenberg Printing**
Visit the National Library of Norway's large collection of manuscripts.

▶**Research Guide to Book History**
Western Connecticut State University has this links page on the history of books.

▶*Secrets of the Dead:* **Mystery of the Black Death**
This PBS site provides a look at the long and deadly history of the bubonic plague.

▶**Treasures in Full: Gutenberg Bible**
On this site, view the British Library's two copies of Johann Gutenberg's Bible.

▶**What Did Gutenberg Invent?**
This BBC Renaissance Secrets Web page tells the history of the printing press.

▶**What People Said About Books in 1498**
This article compares and contrasts the introduction of movable type and computer technology.

alloy—A mixture of metals.

apprentice—A person learning a craft or trade from a master of that craft or trade.

bubonic plague—A fatal disease with painful swelling of the lymph glands and a darkening of the skin.

calligraphy—Handwriting as an art.

chamber pot—A bowl or other type of pot that was used as a toilet before the invention of running water. Often, people would simply empty the contents of their chamber pots into the street. This led to the spread of diseases such as the bubonic plague.

chase—A frame used to hold metal type in place.

convent—A place where nuns live and work.

form—A page of type which has been made secure in a frame and is ready for printing.

guild—A group of merchants or craftsmen, especially before 1500, that worked in the same trade.

guldens—Plural for guilder, a coin formerly used as money in Germany, Austria, and the Netherlands.

illuminated manuscripts—Pages of books decorated with gold or silver and brilliant colors.

indulgences—No longer issued, they were receipts from the Catholic Church issued after a person donated money in exchange for the forgiveness of their sins.

matrix—The receptacle for the molten metal which forms the letter part of the type.

medieval—Of, or relating to the Middle Ages.

Middle Ages—A period of time in European history that lasted from A.D. 500 to 1500.

mint—A place where coins are made.

monasteries—Buildings where monks live and work.

monks—Men who live in a monastery to devote themselves to their religious vows.

parchment—The skin of a sheep or goat, specially dried and prepared, and used in former times for writing on.

patrician—A person descended from the nobility.

pilgrimage—A journey to a holy place, for religious reasons.

printing press—A machine used to push inked metal type against a sheet of paper.

punch—A tool with a raised letter carved at one end.

scribes—People who copy manuscripts by hand.

scriptorium—A room in a monastery for copying, illustrating, reading, and storing manuscripts.

typographic—Relating to typography, or the process of pressing letters to paper to form words or images.

vellum—The best parchment, made from calfskin.

versal—A large, decorative letter at the beginning of a chapter in a book.

Chapter 1. Spreading the Word

1. Elizabeth L. Eisenstein, *The Printing Revolution in Early Modern Europe,* Cambridge University Press, Cambridge, 1993, p. 174.

2. John Man, *Gutenberg: How One Man Remade the World with Words* (New York: John Wiley & Sons, Inc., 2002), pp. 89–90.

3. Ibid., p. 104.

4. Ibid., p. 113.

5. JAARS Museum of the Alphabet, "The Korean Alphabet: On of the World's Most Scientific," *Ancient Alphabets,* 1999–2003, http://www.jaars.org/museum /alphabet/galleries/korean.htm (August 30, 2007).

6. David Owen, *Copies in Seconds* (New York: Simon & Schuster, 2004), p. 16.

7. H. G. Wells, *The Outline of History: Being a Plain History of Life and Mankind* (New York: Doubleday & Company, Inc., 1971), p. 628.

Chapter 2. Johannes Gutenberg: The Early Years

1. Roger B. Beck, Linda Black, Phillip C. Naylor, and Dahia Ibo Shabaka, *World History: Patterns of Interaction* (Evanston, Illinois: McDougal Littell, 1999), p. 357.

2. Michael Worth Davison (Editor), *Everyday Life Through the Ages* (New York: Reader's Digest, 1992), p. 150.

3. John Man, *How One Man Remade the World with Words* (New York: John Wiley & Sons, Inc., 2002), pp. 22–23.

Chapter 3. Gutenberg in Strasbourg

1. John Man, *How One Man Remade the World with Words* (New York: John Wiley & Sons, Inc., 2002), p. 55.

2. Ibid., p. 66.

Chapter 4. Working Toward the Big Breakthrough

1. James Moran, *Printing Presses: History & Development from the Fifteenth Century to Modern Times* (Berkeley and Los Angeles: University of California Press, 1973) p. 18.

2. Ibid., p. 21.

Chapter 5. Europe's First Book Printed With Movable Type

1. John Man, *How One Man Remade the World with Words* (New York: John Wiley & Sons, Inc., 2002), p. 146.

2. Ibid., pp. 175–176.

3. Ibid., p. 182.

4. Ibid., p. 194.

5. Ibid., p. 200.

6. Ibid., p. 212.

7. Ibid., p. 213.

Chapter 6. How Gutenberg's Movable Type Changed the World

1. Will Durant, *The Reformation: A History of European Civilization from Wyclif to Calvin: 1300–1564* (New York: Simon and Schuster, 1957), p. 159.

2. Ibid., p. 159.

3. Elizabeth L. Eisenstein, *The Printing Revolution in Early Modern Europe* (New York: Cambridge University Press, 2005), p. 15.

4. David Owen, *Copies in Seconds* (New York: Simon & Schuster, 2004), pp. 19–20.

5. H. G. Wells, *The Outline of History: Being a Plain History of Life and Mankind* (New York: Doubleday & Company, Inc., 1971), pp. 628–629.

6. Elizabeth L. Eisenstein, *The Printing Revolution in Early Modern Europe* (New York: Cambridge University Press, 2005), p. 171.

7. Ibid., p. 164.

8. Ibid., p. 167.

Crompton, Samuel Willard. *The Printing Press: Transforming the Power of Technology.* Philadelphia: Chelsea House Publishers, 2004.

Heinrichs, Ann. *The Printing Press.* New York: Franklin Watts, 2005.

Koscielniak, Bruce. *Johann Gutenberg and the Amazing Printing Press.* Boston: Houghton Mifflin Co., 2003.

Meltzer, Milton. *The Printing Press.* New York: Benchmark Books, 2004.

Mullins, Lisa. *Inventing the Printing Press.* St. Catharines, Ont.: Crabtree Pub., 2007.

Pollard, Michael. *Johann Gutenberg: Master of Modern Printing.* Woodbridge, Conn.: Blackbirch Press, Inc., 2001.

Powell, Michelle. Printing. Chicago: Heinemann Library, 2000.

Rees, Fran. *Johannes Gutenberg: Inventor of the Printing Press.* Minneapolis: Compass Point Books, 2006.

Tames, Richard. *The Printing Press: A Breakthrough in Communication.* Chicago: Heinemann Library, 2006.

Woods, Michael and Mary B. *The History of Communication.* Minneapolis, Minn.: Twenty-First Century Books, 2006.